# EXCUSE ME, WHAT WAS THAT?

## Confused Recollections of Things That Didn't Go Exactly Right

# EXCUSE ME, WHAT WAS THAT?

## Confused Recollections of Things That Didn't Go Exactly Right

by

Anton Braun Quist

**dilithium Press**
Beaverton, Oregon

10  9  8  7  6  5  4  3  2  1

Library of Congress Catalog Card Number: 82-2502

ISBN 0-88056-076-2

Cover and illustrations: Nate Butler

Printed in the United States of America

dilithium Press
11000 S.W. 11th Street
Beaverton, Oregon 97005

# Quist's Law of Random Perversity

"You never know 'til later."

(The number of variables affecting our enterprises is greater than the rational mind can handle.)

# Quist's Corollary

"In real life, there is no such thing as playing with a full deck."

# Dedication

This one's for

GLENN NORRIS

Who not only has to deal with
this sort of thing
on a daily basis,
but must listen
to the stories again.


With another tip of the hat to

ED DOHERTY

Who should have his name spelled right
at least once, somewhere.

# CHAPTERS

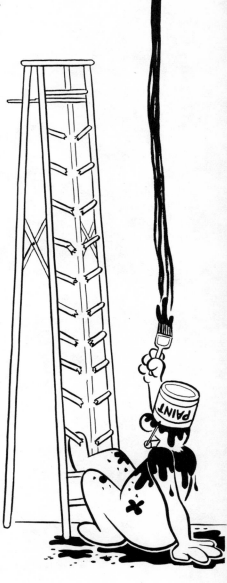

# A Beginning

Why do things go wrong, so aft agly?

Even Murphy's Law is unreliable. Things that can go wrong don't always go wrong, even when they should, when we give them every opportunity, when we go out of our way to fail.

Yes, statistically those people with skill, stamina, wisdom, talent, and helpful friends tend to accomplish more of the things they set out to do than do ignorant, tired, stupid, ungifted loners, but in any given situation the outcome is essentially random.

Why? Profound studies on the perversity of life have given us no satisfactory conclusions, no general revelations. John Gall, in the great tradition of Parkinson and Peter, has systematized an approach to the analysis of systems.* Gall has made valuable contributions to our understanding of organized failure, starting with the pithy consensus of experienced observers that "Things Aren't Working Very Well." That's an important thing to know, and Gall makes the most of it. However, when he is finished, we are still not sure why even governments occasionally do something right, against all odds.

There's a touch of panic in all human endeavor, a drive to be mysterious that flavors all action, and has not yet been accounted for in formulas for predicting results.

---

*Systemantics*, John Gall (Quadrangle, New York, 1975).

Perhaps Canada Bill Jones' Law best catches the spirit of this**: "A Smith and Wesson Beats Four Aces." Suddenly the rules have changed. Most players aren't prepared for the different game, and all plans are irrelevant.

...BEST CATCHES THE SPIRIT...

Therein lies the beauty of this study, the serene conviction that we never have enough information about our complicated world, and never have enough skill to know what will happen in any given venture. There's comfort in that knowledge, a release from the grinding suspicion that we are personally responsible for everything that happens in the universe, whether we're part of the action or not.

But then, there's the sneaking suspicion that an underlying scheme of some sort, not just whimsy, governs our affairs, and we are irresponsible in failing to find it.

The materials offered here, miscellaneous reports of things that didn't go exactly right, are unexplained. They touch on famous people and obscure people, events of some significance and others of no apparent importance,

---

**1,001 Logical Laws (etc.), John Peers, Gordon Bennett (Doubleday, New York, 1979).

but each features that touch of panic that makes life worth living.

Someone may actually derive wisdom from what is of-fered here, probably by accident. All efforts to learn anything from the experience of others have thus far proved inconclusive.

Try your luck.

# Excuse Me, What Was That?

Personal computing is still newsworthy, and attracts excited comment from reporters who don't know a byte from a warthog. Therein lies both opportunity and danger. *Personal* refers here to computer performance in which the system seems to care what happens. Thousands of plain folks are buying small systems these days, determined to wring this sort of performance out of the indifferent hardware.

When you have some technology that really seems to be interested in its user, you're a cinch for good national publicity, true? Yes. In this case, reality is as good as the pipe dream.

The problem is to remember where the line is between technology and show biz. When you step into the limelight, a different set of angels takes over your affairs. The show angels smoke cigars, and laugh a lot, unlike the technical angels, who look worried all the time, and speak exclusively in formulae.

Two of my clients were drawn into the limelight with products that get personal. One is John Peers, whose ADAM computer system (manufactured by Logical Machine Corp.) can be instructed by a naive user in comparatively relaxed English. The other is George Glaser (escaped president of AFIPS), whose product, MIKE, accepts spoken commands, and responds aloud.

... A DIFFERENT SET OF ANGELS TAKES OVER...

(Mr. Glaser was president of Centigram Corp.) When Mr. Peers' computer is equipped with Mr. Glaser's product, a naive user can speak to the system aloud and cause it to operate. Very personal. Intoxicating power.

And so it came to pass that a wise producer of NBC's "Today" show decided that it would be interesting to have somebody with a ready tongue say a few stimulating things about the future of computing early one morning. (What's that laughter? Who's smoking a cigar?)

Doreen Chu, of the "Today" show, was saddled with the task of drawing a computerist into the limelight, and she was steered to John Peers in California. Ms. Chu dangled the bait of six minutes on national television. Mr. Peers did not step delicately across the line from technology to show biz; he *leapt* across.

First, Mr. Peers called me in Albuquerque, that center of advanced technology, show biz, and green chili, where I hunch daily over my typewriter, withdrawn from reality. "Do something appropriate," said Peers, "whatever is necessary. We can tape it here in Sunnyvale, or maybe in Los Angeles, not necessarily in New

York. Whatever they want. I'll be traveling in England or on the Continent if you need me. Ta ta." And off he went.

So, I called Ms. Chu. Six minutes or so would indeed be scheduled, four minutes of jolly conversation in which the future would be revealed in detail, and a couple minutes of demonstration of current miraculous machine capability. Excellent.

One hooker.

"Taped? Oh no, not taped – live. In New York."

Live, alive-o.

"Mr. Peers said that he has a machine that listens to its operator, then talks back. Is that right?"

"Yes. What would the 'Today' show like the conversation between Peers and Machine to be about?"

"You know more about it than we do. Make some specific suggestions."

"Well," said I, warming to the old show biz call, "how about introducing Gene Shallit to MIKE and having the machine say something witty, like 'What a moustache!' MIKE could say 'pretty lady' at the mention of Jane Pauley."

No, this should be serious, demonstrating something important about the future.

Nondialing telephones? Just tell the phone who it is you want to call?

No, they were tired of telephone talk. Something else.

Okay, I'd write a couple of little routines to consider. Did they really want the whole computer system or just the speech-recognition-and-response black box?

It wasn't really necessary to drag 700 lb. ADAM to New York. MIKE was sufficiently charming along. Super. I knew we could send at least two working MIKE's. My theory is that the guardian angels like to spice up show biz demonstrations of working hardware by casting a spell so that 53% of the demonstrations fail at the critical moment, increasing the entertainment value of the events.

So, with MIKE's enough to handle the angels, I put
together a couple of routines. One was a security
system.

"Knock, knock," says Peers.

"Who's there?" says MIKE.

"John Peers," says Peers.

"What company?" says MIKE.

"Logical Machine Corporation."

"Phone number?"

. . . and so on. . . the notion being that MIKE asks questions at random that only the real John Peers would be
able to answer promptly. MIKE might have 50 such questions in memory, with a checklist of answers. If the guy
at the door answers correctly in John's voice, MIKE accepts him as the genuine article.

"What's the password?" says MIKE.

"Swordfish."

"Why, John Peers, is that you?"

"Yes, indeed."

"Come in."

. . . and MIKE unlocks the door. Corny routine, but swift
and clear in its purpose.

The other routine did involve both MIKE and ADAM. It
was an inventory-taking procedure in which a
storekeeper calls out information aloud in response to
prompting from MIKE. Very businesslike, in spite of
MIKE's wisecracks.

"Today" show hated the routines. "We need something
the housewife can understand," said Ms. Chu.

Any other hints?

No, I should make more specific suggestions.

How about a routine on automatic shopping. You tell
the system what you need from the store; it tells you the
cost and what's in stock, then orders from the store's
computer automatically.

That might be nice, but it shouldn't be frivolous. Practical, useful, informative. Those were the keys.

Righto.

"By the way," said Ms. Chu, "they want to know if the computer can sing."

"Sing?"

"Yes."

"Um... not very well," I said, wondering what had suddenly become of practical, useful, and informative.

"That's what I thought," said Ms. Chu with relief in her voice. "We now have the appearance set for Tuesday, the 9th of May. Will that do?"

It would do. The wandering Mr. Peers could get back from Europe for the occasion.

I ground out a couple of minutes of uplifting shopping dialogue between John and MIKE. Panic was manifest in Sunnyvale, since customers were demanding delivery of all the MIKE's that could be made, but...

On Saturday, April 29, Mr. Peers called from London to find out how things were going. He decided that MIKE/ADAM should be on the show, not just MIKE. "Tell them in Sunnyvale that we need both. Keep me informed. My secretary will be reaching me in Amsterdam. Ta ta." Something must have twanged the cable we were using, or bumped the satellite. I thought I heard laughter from afar.

The MIKE/ADAM routine was technically practical, and I had seen people control ADAM by speaking to MIKE, but there were still a few bugs. One knew it would all work perfectly, but when?

At least 20 people were involved by now, and several of them were calling NBC independently to ask critical questions. ("When can we get in to set up? Not until you sweep John Chancellor and the remnants of the "Evening News" out of that studio about eight the evening before? If the equipment arrives on Monday morning, does it have to sit out on Fifth Avenue until Mr. Chancellor is through? You mean we can't rehearse with the "Today" people until six in the morning? We draw under 20 amps of 110 and we wish we had a clean line. You can give us a thousand amps? Wow!")

Mr. Peers was scheduled to stop in at Ms. Chu's office on Friday, the 5th, to discuss the script of the demo. John had never seen the script, of course. He phoned me at Albuquerque sunrise that day to say: "I'm at the Plaza Hotel, and there's no bloody script here. Read it to me."

I crawled out of bed, found my glasses, hunted for the script, fell asleep briefly at my desk, crawled back to the phone, and fumbled through a recitation.

Mr. Peers loved it, loved it.

"Good Lord," he said, "can the system really do all that?"

"Theoretically, yes. We won't know in practice until it's too late."

"Marvelous," said the adventure-loving Monty Python of the Computer Industry, and went off to do his thing.

MIKE/ADAM worked perfectly for the first time on Saturday. Peers rehearsed a few times over the weekend in California, then sent people and equipment to New York in a swarm. Secure in the knowledge that "Today" would settle for MIKE alone in case the Mafia hijacked ADAM at the airport, and we couldn't raise the ransom in time, George Glaser headed east with two MIKE's under his arms.

The fellows galloped into the studio on Chancellor's heels, and had the sytem operating before midnight. MIKE/ADAM worked like a champ. "The system was working so well," reports Glaser, "that it was a great distraction for the crew. They kept playing with it. There were a few small hitches, of course. After we had the 700 lb. machine working, the director discovered that he couldn't cover it in that position, and we tore it down to move ten feet.' (Laughter and smoke rings.)

The reporters and guests came in about six. Mr. Peers (who was a professional piano player at one time) sat at ADAM's keyboard to render a few routines for Sammy Cahn and Alan Jay Lerner. The distinguished songwriters were there in celebration of Irving Berlin's 90th birthday. (Is *that* why Ms. Chu asked about singing?)

Just before airtime, Peers retaught MIKE the commands he wanted the machine to recognize, a three- or four-minute task. If the operator's voice changes significantly, the machine may not identify him. Peers had slept about three hours in the last 50, was still waiting for the jet lag to catch him, and was about to perform for the biggest audience of his life. He wanted MIKE to know about any stress in his voice.

The recognition vocabulary is stored in MIKE's random access memory.

Volatile RAM.

The phrases MIKE speaks aloud are also recorded in RAM.

Tom Brokaw wondered if the system could respond to him. Yes, there were three recognition and response slots open, so they quickly worked out a routine in which Peers introduced Brokaw to MIKE/ADAM, and the two exchanged pleasantries for a few seconds.

All set.

"Hey," said somebody in the control booth. "That machine must be putting funny signals on our lines. The automatic switcher doesn't work when the computer's on. You'll have to turn it off during the first part of the show." And he reached for a switch.

Peers, Glaser, and their crew flung themselves on the man and the machines. Switchoff meant that ADAM and MIKE would forget everything they knew, with no time for retraining. STOP!

Miraculously, he stopped. The stuff in RAM was saved. On with the show.

The little introductory discussion went well when the time came, and Peers turned confidently to ADAM.

"Good morning, ADAM," said Peers.

"Good morning, John," said MIKE/ADAM in George Glaser's voice, since it was George who had recorded the responses.

"I want to buy some groceries," said Peers. "Take a shopping list for me."

... FLUNG THEMSELVES ON THE MAN ...

"What items?" said MIKE/ADAM.

"Fresh butter."

"Fresh butter," said MIKE/ADAM, and displayed "Butter...$1.45" on ADAM's screen.

"Is it that much?" said Peers, expecting MIKE/ADAM to reply with: "It's gone up."

Instead, the machine said: "Excuse me, what was that?" That's what MIKE/ADAM is supposed to say when it doesn't understand a command clearly.

"Is it that much?" said Peers with dignity.

"Excuse me, what was that?"

"Is it that much?"

"Excuse me, what was that?"

"ADAM doesn't seem to like the hot lights," said Peers thoughtfully.

"Excuse me, what was that?"

"Be quiet, ADAM," said Mr. Peers.

"Excuse me, what was that?"

"Well, let's talk about some other things." said Mr. Brokaw, and he asked a question.

"Excuse me, what was that?" said MIKE/ADAM.

Peers launched into a discussion of Mr. Brokaw's question. Poor old MIKE/ADAM was by now firmly stuck in a loop. Every few seconds, George Glaser's voice would pipe up "Excuse me, what was that?" in a pathetic, demented cycle. After about three minutes of this torment, Mr. Glaser himself was on his hands and knees, creeping behind Peers and Brokaw, behind MIKE/ADAM, heading for the loudspeaker on the floor. He was planning to rip out its little wires. You don't get to be a consultant, a corporation president, and leader of the American Federation of Information Processing Societies by wallowing in indecision. George was bent on murder.

Peers, meanwhile, had no operating control of the system from the keyboard, that being one of the refinements overlooked in the previous week's frenzy. Rigid self-discipline also prevented him from turning off the master switch on ADAM, since this scrambles the innards in unhandy ways. Brokaw had no such inhibition.

"Maybe we should switch this off," he said, and did it.

"Excuse me," said MIKE/ADAM, and fainted.

Mr. Glaser did not creep into national view. Mr. Peers did not cry on camera, but spoke winningly of better things to come. A smell of cigar smoke and a sound of giggling filled the air.

After the commercial break, Peers and Brokaw chatted on for an unscheduled five minutes in a segment that is not seen everywhere around the country. In Albuquerque they opted for local news, and I chewed my rug in ignorance of the relaxed exchange.

When MIKE/ADAM got home, the system worked flawlessly once more. Was it the lights? Were signals from the automatic switcher leaking in? The scientists are working on that. Overall, of course, it was the move from technology to show biz that caused the system to lose its marbles at the critical time.

It *is* only a paper moon in show biz, not only because the producers are too cheap to use the real thing, but because the real thing probably won't work when the curtain rises.

Indeed, the panic of MIKE/ADAM was so genuine, and so appealing in human terms, that Peers, Glaser, et al. have been awash in sympathy. No mocking laughter, except from above. The "Today" show folks were almost as disappointed as Peers, and have extended an invitation to come back when MIKE/ADAM are feeling better. Not as good an effect as we had hoped, but better by far than we feared. Trouper Peers came through in style.

Certainly our convictions were reconfirmed. Personal computing *is* noteworthy.

"Excuse me, what was that?"

## POSTSCRIPT TO EXCUSE ME

It has been a while, now, and one may well ask (one *does* ask) what the problem was that day in New York. Did the searching scientists ever figure it out?

Yes, they did, and were embarrassed as ever to discover the cause of the problem. Not hot lights, not the bumpiness of the ride to New York, not spurious signals on the lines, none of those things that can be blamed on somebody else. It was a programming error. Aaaaha!

MIKE requires training, must be taught those phrases he is to recognize. When MIKE is to learn a new set of phrases for recognition, the old recognition vocabulary is erased, forgotten. Or, if MIKE/ADAM is switched off, the old stuff is forgotten, and new training is required. Volatile memory, and all that.

The folks were up all night, setting up, training, retraining, switching off, starting over, moving about, growing tired. Most of the night, ADAM was switched on and off to meet current needs. At each switch-off MIKE properly forgot the old vocabulary.

As airtime approached, and people grew tense, ADAM was not switched off. Mr. Peers made three passes at training MIKE in the half-hour before airtime, right up to that last-second crisis.

And therein lay the fatal flaw. The frenzied week's development had failed to supply ADAM with a software command that erased MIKE's memory as it should have been erased. All training between switchoffs was *cumulative*. In fact, it is quite practical to teach MIKE the words "Stop, Halt," and "Arrete," not to mention "Whoa" and "unh-unh," on the same channel. This allows MIKE to accept the "stop" command in any language or style that is likely to occur to a desperate operator under stress. All those sounds produce the same response.

There's a limit to this technique, though. After enough training with different words on the same channel, everything begins to sound alike to MIKE. The pattern he's supposed to identify blurs, and ceases to be distinctly different from other things. Even the same words, repeated many times in training, grow indistinct, because each rendering is slightly different from the others, especially when the renderer is semi-conscious from fatigue.

The last three times John trained MIKE, the training was overlaid on what was already there. Poor old MIKE just didn't know what to think, and did what he was supposed to do. Hearing sound apparently intended for judgement, but not sharply identified, MIKE/ADAM said "Excuse me, what was that?" in all sincerity.

A programming bug.

Well, what did we expect?

# Secret Processes

While many projects and products fail for unaccountable and unexpected reasons, many others *work* for unaccountable and unexpected reasons. On behalf of the yet unidentified theorist who will some day find a sensible way to deal with these matters, here are some things that work for no good reasons.

There were the people who manufactured traveling wave tubes for some years with great success, and at an attractive profit. What's a traveling wave tube? Oh, it's something to do with radar, and very high frequency communications stuff. The TWT's pumped electrons into one end of a glass tube, did something useful to them, and pumped them out the other end to be used in mysterious ways.

A key feature of the TWT was a wire coil, corkscrewing its way through the tube. This helix was a picky thing to make, and had to be placed just-so to work. This company had reduced the mechanical assembly of the product from an art to a systematic science, and had documented every step of the procedure so a fairly smart monkey could handle the job with a bit of training.

Except that, one day, the company could not make any TWT's that worked. Extraordinary measures were taken to make the practices on the assembly line conform rigidly with the known process. Still, no working tubes came off the line. Every one failed its tests. As the days passed, and the customers began to moan and holler about deliveries, management buckled down to a serious technical study of the materials, the test equipment, everything that might affect the manufacture of working products.

At last it occurred to somebody that the screeching halt in production coincided with the departure of one employee, a lady who had quietly been working on the line for a few years. They fetched her back with entreaties and offers of money, to rejoin the line for an experiment. Sure enough, working traveling wave tubes began to flow from the line.

They grouped around here, watched her every move, checked her actions against the production manual. Yes, yes, yes, yup, that's right, that too, yes, yes. Wait!

Wait?

"Do that again."

"Do what?"

"What you just did?"

"What did I do?"

"Start the process again. Yes, yes, yes. . . stop hold it right there. What are you doing now?"

The lady studied her position.

"Oh," she said. "You wonder why I have my thumbnail stuck in between the end of the helix and the next element?"

"Yes."

"Gee, I don't know. I've just always done it. That's how I locate the helix, I guess, never really thought about it. The tubes work when I do this, and I've never had any reason to change."

They used a micrometer on her thumbnail, prepared a gauge of the same thickness, and used it to make traveling wave tubes that worked. So much for science.

Same thing at the integrated circuit factory. Suddenly, they couldn't make circuits that worked. The problem

... A MICROMETER ON HER THUMBNAIL ...

correlated with the sickness of an employee at one point
in the process. This employee was a smoker, given to
sneaking cigarettes in a forbidden area when the
foreman wasn't looking.

The smoke in the otherwise superclean area was just
enough to contaminate the semiconductor materials so
they worked. Once again, to quote sage Ed Whitaker,
"fear and superstition triumphed over science and
technology."

And there were the guys at the lens factory.

Optics is an arcane art, a mystery barely subject to
human influence, and the optical works provide us with
many useful stories.

In this case two full-grown men spent eight hours a
day for two years, using a Comptometer machine (for
you young sprats, this was a marvelous mechanical
calculator whose power held a generation of folks in
awe) to calculate the specifications of a new microscope
lens.

No simple task. This was an eleven element lens, a so-
called 43x high-dry objective.

"ONCE AGAIN, FEAR AND SUPERSTITION HAD TRIUMPHED OVER SCIENCE AND TECHNOLOGY."

Time out for optics: High-dry? Well, the objective lens of a microscope is the one down there at the bottom next to the thing you are looking at. The greater its power, the closer it has to be to the object. That means *very* close as you go up in power. Thousandths of an inch. You can't get any light on the thing you are looking at; the lens tends to hit the object before you can get close enough to look down in a crack, and all that. Troublesome. This distance between the lens and the thing you are looking at is called the *working distance*, reasonably enough. (Through some black magic, we once built a microscope that could resolve a thousandth of a millimeter at a working distance of six inches, so you could look right down inside things. Don't ask. It wasn't easy, and not much fun.)

One way to increase the working distance is to use an *oil immersion* lens. If you look through something more dense than air, the focal length of the lens is decreased a bit, so you actually have more working distance, and can hold focus. It's a mess. You literally put a drop of oil on what you're looking at, and run the lens down so it's in contact with the drop of oil.

A *high-dry* objective gives high magnification (in this case forty-three times) and doesn't need an oil drop. The development of a good 43x high-dry was wonderful, applauded by the manufacturer and by the customers alike.

The chaps finished their arduous design work, and sent the specs out to the production people.

In due course, the lens came back to them in finished form. It was a masterpiece. Its performance exceeded their wildest hopes. It was perfect.

The second one couldn't be focused on anything, and neither could the third. They felt that a trend had been established, so they threw an armed guard around lens number one, and examined it in exhaustive detail to see why it worked.

Turned out that somebody in the production department had made one of the elements out of a piece of glass with the wrong index of refraction, not what the plans called for.

After two years of superhuman design and calculation, the first lens worked only because somebody made a mistake in production. Did they struggle over this, and fit the hardware to the original design? They did not. They changed the plans to fit what worked, thanked Heaven for large favors, and manufactured a lot of lenses that actually worked. There may have been some soft crying in quiet corners about all the backbreaking labor that went for naught, but a winner is a winner.

And there was the inertial guidance system critical to the performance of many U.S. space vehicles. A visitor was shown the working device and its specifications, and he was filled with wonder.

"Why, that's fiendishly clever," said he, "but very peculiar. I can't imagine how the design occurred to you. It looks as if two of the three accelerometers are fairly good, and identical, while the whole thing hinges on the super performance of the third accelerometer, which must be ten times better than the other two. Remarkable."

"Yes, we're pleased that it works."

"How did you find a supplier for accelerometers with those exact characteristics?"

"Well, we make them ourselves."

"An astounding feat of design. How do you manage it?"

"By accident, actually. The fact is that we set out to make one very good accelerometer around which we could design the inertial guidance system. When we began to manufacture the things, we found that two thirds of them weren't very good, didn't come up to our planned specs, but that one out of three, on the average, is ten times better than the others, truly marvelous. So, we designed around what we had."

"Why are the bad ones bad?"

"We haven't the faintest idea."

"Why are the good ones good?"

"We haven't the faintest idea; they're all made on the same line in exactly the same way. Some are great, some are not."

"Is there any reason to suppose this will continue?"

"We haven't the faintest idea."

"Don't you worry?"

"Yes."

"What do you plan to do?"

"Hope it continues."

They did, and it did.

During World War II, a great deal of equipment was built for airplanes that operated on 28 volts of DC current, nominally. Historical accident, really. There's nothing all that attractive about 28 volt DC stuff, but there it was. If you are flying around in an airplane with the appropriate generator, that power is readily available. (Actually, since engine speeds varied appreciably, a range of 22 to 28 volts was normal.) If you are working in a repair and maintenance shop for the airplane electrical equipment, you must somehow convert 110 volts

AC to what you want, or keep an airplane engine running a generator in the back room. Inconvenient.

This was before solid state electronics. Nothing was easy. Whipping out an inverter for this was a big task. However, there was a way — and oddly, it was really based on solid state electronics before the transistor.

Since about 1870, the *electric eye* has been commercially available. The electric eye involves coating an iron plate with selenium, and coating the selenium with silver. What you create this way is a *rectifier* that can give you DC out from AC in. Handy, also light sensitive in a useful way, hence the name.

It was not tough to build a stack of these things that would give the maintenance and repair people power for their work. Given the probability that airplanes would be important in the war, action was taken to increase the production of electric eyes.

The National Academy of Sciences sent nosey scientific agents of the government out to the grubby old factory where the objects were made, and grilled the managers to learn their quaint ways, and systematize the process. The managers did not all enjoy being questioned, corrected, patronized, and snubbed by the agents of the central government, but they provided all of the production specifications and procedures.

The whippersnappers followed the instructions, and couldn't make any electric eyes that would work. They went back for more information, indignantly insisting that they be told everything. One young chap in the party of raiders was not important enough to attend the serious meetings with the management of the firm, but wandered around the plant, fascinated. He chatted with people, admired their vats and flagons, petted the dog, and enjoyed himself hugely.

After the shouting died down in the meeting room,and the experts were preparing to go off for another try at electric eye production, an oldtimer in the back room took the unimportant visitor aside.

"You're such a nice young fellow," said he, "that we've decided to let you in on something the management doesn't know about here. There's a step in the production of these things that was never written down."

"Really?"

"Yes, and if it will be any help to you, we'll tell you about it."

"I'd certainly like to know."

"Follow me."

And they stepped out the back door, taking the path through the weeds to the privy. A vile tin can sat out there next to the outhouse, and the oldtimer pointed out that it was half full of some fluid.

"When it's full, we dump about all of it into one of the chemical processing vats in there."

"Is it what I think?"

"Sure, it's a bucket of piss."

"Why do you do that?"

"Well, if we do it, we can make those electric eyes work. If we don't do it, we can't make them work."

"Does it matter who contributes to that bucket?"

"Doesn't seem to. Lots of people have been contributors over the years..."

... A VILE TIN CAN...

"How did you figure out that this was the thing to do?"

"Nobody really knows. It's just sort of a tradition."

"And it's all right with you if I give this information to the people I work for?"

"You go ahead and do that."

He did it.

We won the war.

Every little bit helps.

An observation: Rigidly controlled situations, in which effective measures are taken to prevent anything bad from happening, also prevent anything good from happening. It remains to be seen whether Ralph Nader and his associates can win a war or not.

Fortunately, fear and superstition **will** triumph over science and technology often enough to permit survival.

# Up, Up and Away

Helicopters are all very well, but they have not developed yet into Everyman's Model T of the Air, despite vigorous efforts at development and promotion of personal whirlybirds.

A California chap, otherwise a sane and distinguished technical man, developed a truly tiny chopper that straps to the user's back. Powered by something like an outboard motor, this device is not weighed down unduly by landing gear, a body shell to protect the flyer from the elements, navigation instruments, and other luxuries. You just strap the thing on, pull the cord, and sail away. The happy inventor envisions hordes of commuters, carrying their lunchbags and briefcases, flying from the suburbs to offices in the cities.

Fascinating vision: thousands of people dangling from the whirling blades, crowding the flyways like cars on the freeways, clipping a tree here, dropping through a roof there. It stirs the blood just to think of it.

The inventor recognized the limitations of the device, and proposed a modest early application: never mind flying all the way to the office; just make it from home down to the train station. Park the gadget at the station, and use it to get home again in the evening. He longed to make an impressive demonstration, but he had not yet caught the full attention of the aeronautical authorities, and he was afraid that if he roused the sleeping dog, it

.. COMMUTERS FLYING FROM THE SUBURBS ...

would forbid him to do what he wanted in the way of a show.

At last he determined to sneak the show. He waited for a foggy morning, not too long a wait in his neighborhood, and strapped on his flying machine. Up he went, through the murk, above the fog layer into the glorious sunshine. He churned away, following tall landmarks, identified the train station, and swooped in.

The regular commuters were standing on the platform, absently drinking coffee, and reading their papers, when a strange chopping sound reached them faintly, then more intensely. A startling spectacle appeared to them as a maniac dropped from the gloomy sky into their midst, feet and arms dangling grotesquely. The maniac landed on the platform, looked around, shouted triumphantly, revved up his motor, and swirled away into the fog once again before anybody could react. Success!

Of course, the police station happened to be across the street from the railroad station/helicopter pad, and even the cops noticed the unusual landing through the gloom. Inquiries were made; the local technical nut is not too hard to identify, and the civil authorities responsible for limits on flying paid him a visit. Didn't work out too bad, really. They let him fly his gadget as a duly licensed experimental craft to a height of not more than fifty feet in a particular open area. The local cops were encouraged to shoot him out of the air if he strayed from that little area. From time to time, he goes out for a spin.

The commuters are waiting a little more alertly for action at the station, but nothing that good has ever come back.

Helicopters have often been more troublesome. They've been around for a long time, but not always in practical form. It wasn't until about 1950 that a major American aircraft company was ready to build helicopters in practical commercial form.

Indeed, the project had dragged on for quite some time, frustrating a lot of people while the engineers struggled with endless bugs in the system.

The experimental craft sat out on the pad, but the engineers couldn't quite bring themselves to let anybody fly the beast, even tethered. They were bothered by some things that they just couldn't explain clearly. Wait, just wait.

At last the test pilot scheduled for the first experiments couldn't stand it any longer. He stamped in one morning, raising a fuss, and declaring that he would fly the machine that day, no matter what. Never mind any engineering mumbo-jumbo, it was flying time. He led a procession out to the chopper, and got it set to fly while crews scurried around to document the event.

He climbed in, fired the machine up, put the gas to it, and rose gracefully from the pad. Grit triumphed over mere engineering. Up, up, a few feet, a few more.

Then the engineers had their innings. When a long blade of a chopper swings around, it pushes on the air. It pushes some air down. When the machine is close to the ground, the pushed air hits the ground, and bounces back up. There comes a point when the upward-bound air from one blade exactly catches the following blade. This creates what is called a *ground effect* by some skilled in the aeronautical arts.

In this case, the effect was to cause the helicopter to bounce up and down somewhat. More than somewhat. Rapidly, and with great violence. Enough violence to loosen the nasty-tempered test pilot from his comfortable seat.

As the craft came down on one of its excursions, he was still rising up from his seat. He slipped up next to the hub between the blades. That in itself was no great hardship, because the blades weren't really moving very fast in the center. He just folded over the blade next to the hub. The excitement came after that.

As the blade moved on, the pilot began to slide out from the hub, out to where the blade was moving faster . . . and faster. In the full view of the admiring engineers, the pilot was centrifuged out from the helicopter, off into the air, down onto the pavement. He skipped like a flat pebble across a pond until he fetched up forcefully against a wire fence.

Beautiful.

It looked just as good on the films. Bounce, bounce, bounce. The engineers were gratified beyond measure, not only because they had been vindicated in their esti-

... THE ENGINEERS WERE GRATIFIED BEYOND MEASURE.

mation that this was a bad day to fly a helicopter, but also because they had learned a lot from the test. They promptly made some changes, and figured out an approach to getting the helicopter into the air without launching the pilot to the moon.

Oh, and the pilot? He showed up again the following morn, patched together, bandaged, boiling with rage, swearing that he would fly that helicopter *today*! And he did, strapped firmly in his seat.

# Our Loyal Staff
# is Waiting...

The bright young businessmen got the money together, and bought out the old line optical company. A coup, it was. With those long-neglected resources, their shiny new MBA degrees, and adequate capital, they were a cinch to become a hot new growth company.

To spread the cheer all around among the employees, they even caused a fresh layer of light, green paint to be spread over the grimy, greasy, depressing, dingy old walls of the plant, and installed new lights, so the place was pleasant and encouraging.

Orders flowed in.

The shop was instructed to produce a run of lenses that had for years been a mainstay of the company's business, one of their old, reliable products. Some time passed, and none of these lenses appeared on the shipping dock. An inquiry was sent back to the shop. "When will the lenses be ready?"

Never.

"But..."

The company no longer had the specifications for manufacture of the lenses, didn't know how to make them.

"But, we've been making them for years. Surely we can still do that."

No, the plans were gone.

Fact is, the specs had been written on the walls around the benches of the guys who were doing the work. All sorts of handy reference notes were on the walls, but some fool had come along and put green paint all over everything.

"Why didn't you say something?"

Nobody had asked. Damnfool upstarts. Think they know everything.

... SOME FOOL HAD PUT GREEN PAINT ALL OVER EVERYTHING.

The military negotiated a contract with the firm to make some lenses. The contract was novel in one respect: it required that the lenses be glued in the mounts with epoxy. That was not traditional. All dyed-in-the-wool optical people know that God intended for lenses to be held in place with shellac (or in certain cases with Canada Balsam), not with any newfangled stuff.

Management sent the order back to the shop. The lenses were produced and delivered. The military sent them back after the usual rigorous inspection. "No, no," they said, "you have used shellac in these things. You are supposed to use epoxy."

Management took the specs out to the shop, and discussed the matter with the employees, providing them with a ready supply of epoxy, and checking to see that they knew how to use it.

The military sent the resulting lenses back, owing to another bad case of shellac-employment.

This time, management gathered up all the shellac in the plant, and disposed of it, so no untoward accident should occur again.

It occurred again. This time a serious investigation was launched, and it turned up some interesting facts. There existed in the company an organization of old timers, The Thirty Year Club. The greybeards of The Thirty Year Club had foreseen this crisis. They knew that sooner or later the Devil would whisper wicked suggestions to the young managers, causing them to abandon shellac in favor of immoral substances like epoxy. In anticipation of the evil time, they had, with their own personal funds, laid in a fifty-five gallon drum of shellac, roughly a thousand year supply the way they used it. When the official company supply was confiscated, they tapped their own private reserve.

... A THOUSAND YEAR SUPPLY...

"My God," commented a consultant, "that's enough shellac to cover everything from here to Madagascar! You'd better think of some other approach to this problem. Those people are at least as smart and resourceful as you are, and they are necessary to this business. Their skill is largely what you purchased."

The handwriting was on the wall, if you'll pardon the reference, and management found another approach. They set up a parallel production line, with new employees under new foremen to produce non-tradional products. This activity was not outstandingly profitable.

# Obsolescence

Specialists have a special problem. If their specialty goes out of style, so do they. When the chemical etching process for producing plates that would print real photographs in newspapers first appeared, there was a wave of suicides around the world among the chaps who made a profession of engraving simulations of photographs for the papers by hand. A shame.

An artist dropped in at a Hollywood studio that produces television commercials. He carried a portfolio with him, and said that he was an animator looking for work. Lot of turnover in that business as people go from studio to studio, following the work, and a good man is always welcome.

Experience?

Lots. Years at Disney.

Ever done any commercials?

Well, no, but lots of movies.

Animals?

Not many.

People?

Few.

Backgrounds?

Very few.

What then?

He was a specialist.

In what?
Water.
Water?
Moving water.
Oh, yeah?

A SPECIALIST IN WATER.

Sure, when Bambi runs through the stream, drops of water splash here and there. When it rains, the water drops fall on the leaves, drip, collect in pools, form streams, go here and there, glistening and sparkling. Moving water.

Disney isn't doing much water these days?

Not much.

Well, unh...there just wasn't all that much call for detailed water in television commercials at that time... but...leave an address, and if any water work came up...

And then there was the armory where they made military rifles. It's considered a good thing for rifle barrels to be straight. Not just sort of straight, but really straight.

A highly skilled expert was needed to look down each barrel and judge its straightness. Was it really straight? If not, how crooked was it? And where was it crooked?

Could it be straightened, or should it be rejected completely?

If it could be straightened, then the inspector himself would do the job, using special tools and the skills acquired in a career of making rifle barrels straight. The expert in this art held a position of honor and dignity much esteemed in the small world of rifle-makers. Apprentices yearned for the time of full acceptance into the ranks of master rifle-barrel straighteners.

In one large armory, a score of masters sat on high stools at a big table to which the barrels were brought crooked, and from which they were taken, straight. The room was not noisy. There was a certain style, solemnity, and serenity in the activity.

Next to each high stool bearing a full fledged master, sat an apprentice on a *low* stool. The apprentice helped the master, learned from him, catered to his needs, and looked forward with burning intensity to acquisition of a high stool and an apprentice of his own.

Full grown men served as low-stool apprentices for an average of fifteen years, acquiring the skill and the style, waiting for folks to topple off high stools, and create openings.

Then one day a system was installed that would straighten rifle barrels without stools. The job no longer existed for a man. The specialty was gone, gone in a twinkling, erased, unmourned by the populace at large.

The apprentices who had labored for fifteen years, who cast their longing eyes daily on the swaying and faintness of masters on the high stools had no place to look forward to. Looking back in nostalgia at the good old days on a low stool must not have been greatly satisfying.

The closing bell that Fate rang in the stool room was deafening.

Old gag: A want ad—Astronomer Wanted.
Must be willing to work nights.

Really, most astronomical observation is done via photography these days, and the old vision of a guy peering through a big telescope through a crack in the roof is largely imaginary.

But not completely. There's a good bit of eyeball work still done, and good night vision is essential.

... A GOOD BIT OF EYEBALL WORK.

People who want to see things through telescopes while looking off in the darkness try to avoid lights for some period of time before looking through the lens, and this presents a problem. An astronomer at work does a lot of measuring and calculating, and it's impractical to make notes on a lighted piece of paper, then look back in the glass.

One astronomer made himself into a worker without peer in his chosen field by memorizing all of the logarithms he needed to do his calculations, thus reducing the amount of bookwork and exposure to bright lights by a significant amount. His productivity climbed dramatically. He memorized about a hundred thousand different logarithms out to eight digits, each. Magnificent.

Then the electronic calculator came upon the scene, and his distinction, except as a parlor performer, waned.

Easy come, easy go.

# The In-Line Computer

"I know what *on-line* means, and I know what *off-line* means when we're talking about computer systems," said the Export Marketing Manager for the U.S. computer company, "but they've got me beat this time; I have no idea what an *in-line* computer system is. Our Japanese distributor is demanding design changes to convert our product to an in-line computer. We have exchanged twenty telexes on the subject. It's driving me nuts."

The company's product, in the mid-seventies, was a splendid small computer for business with a printer, a video display, and a big disc memory, all housed in a handsome L-shaped desk. A beautiful system, with technical innovations of stunning virtue, but unsatisfactory to the Japanese.

Well, if you want something done right, you have to do it yourself, right? That dumb Yankee manager didn't understand plain Japanese, even when it was properly translated. An in-line system has all its elements in a line, not built into a piece of furniture that has an L sticking right out in the middle of the room. In Japan, rooms are small, and proper thinking leads one to design systems that huddle unobtrusively against one wall, leaving the middle of the room for more important functions.

(Besides, the Japanese distributor also represented the firm that made the printer that lived on that L, and couldn't see any point in importing the complete system, when it was so easy to put a cheaper printer on its own stand at the end of the desk.)

It boiled down to a negotiation. The distributor demanded to buy the computer with no furniture at all; he'd build his own. Well, O.K. The Export Manager reduced the system price by $150, and sent the elements without the desk.

After some confusion that did not produce the desired furniture in Japan, the distributor decided to order desks after all. The desk-without-computer to go with the elements he had was now quoted at $900. The distributor accepted this painful reality, and hatched his own plan.

When the first sytem-with-desk was assembled and operating in Tokyo, thirty-seven engineers trooped in to watch a carpenter re-design the stupid Yankee furniture.

The carpenter sawed the offending L off the desk, stroke by stroke, to the quiet satisfaction of the onlookers. At last, he cut through the final quarter-inch of the L. . .and the remainder of the desk, with the active display and the whirling big disc, toppled over on the concrete with a shattering crash.

Thirty-seven engineers leapt forward to right the machine, and determine the cause of the disaster. The cause was straightforward, really. Somewhat to their disappointment, the machine had not been pushed over by the lowly carpenter; it had fallen of its own weight when the balancing L was removed.

Since they were standing there in a closely-knit group anyway, the alert technical staff redesigned the system on the spot. They moved one leg from the middle to the side of the desk, and added another at the other side. Balance. Excellent.

They examined the area where the L had been sawed away, and decided that it should be covered with a nice wooden panel. . . as also should the large hole in the side of the desk that had been left for the purpose of admitting the cables from the printer that was no longer on the L.

You may think these things could have been considered in advance, or might, indeed, have been dealt with more calmly and effectively by one man at a drawing board after the fact. But, as we have observed, there were thirty-seven engineers and a carpenter, all dressed up, and determined to accomplish something.

The committee invented, then and there, a plain panel to cover the flaws generated by the earlier action with the saw. There was some difficulty in securing the panel to the desk without defacing the existing Formica, but it was tacked gingerly in place.

The thirty-eight guys backed away to admire their handiwork. They Saw That It Was Good, and decreed that this would be the way all future systems were to be altered. They marched away to their well-earned sake and fish eyes with a corporate sense of achievement.

THEY SAW THAT IT WAS GOOD.

They sold a bunch of 'em, and the design looked remarkably good, even with the printer at a different height on its hideous stand, placed properly in-line with the desk.

Oh yeah, one thing: for years now, everytime a customer steps up to examine the work of his operator at the machine, and absent-mindedly leans on the desk, that panel drops off with a crash that scares them both out of a year's growth.

Ah teamwork. Up your zaibatsu!

A footnote—

The dumb Yankee manufacturer, controlling his sorrow over the desecration of his product, gained some satisfaction in Japan after all.

He and the Export Manager visited the distributor in Tokyo, and were teasing him about his entertaining pronunciation of English, working as he did with neither an "r" or an "l" in his own language.

The chap bore the teasing with good-humored restraint, but remarked seriously that the Japanese can do anything they set their minds to, if they consider it important. Indeed, he said, the waiters in the Western-style restaurant where they were dining at the moment could handle English, Spanish and German with perfect fluency, switching from one to another without missing a beat.

Properly abashed by this news, the Yankees finished their main course in silence, and inquired of the waiter about dessert.

"We have pie and cheese."

What kind of cheese?

"Two kinds. We have Blie," said the waiter crisply to the awestricken visitors, "and Brue."

# The Hindenburg Syndrome

Otmar Stuetzer is the only man we know who actually worked on the Hindenburg.

"Otmar, the movie about the Hindenburg was on the other night, and the story suggests that the ship was sabotaged by a crew member. Do you know what the Germans really thought about it at the time? Why did it really go down?"

"You are talking to the secretary of the committee that investigated the affair for the German government."

"You?"

"Yes. I was present during all of the meetings. You know what the secretary of a committee is, don't you?"

"Tell us."

"The secretary is the guy who sits there, and writes down everything with a big fountain pen, and keeps his trap shut."

"And what did they decide?"

"They decided to tell the world that it was all the fault of the Americans, who wouldn't let them have any helium, and who forced them to use hydrogen."

"Yes, but what happened?"

"If we had used helium, we wouldn't have made it half way across the Atlantic, let alone all the way to New Jersey. That thing leaked. Helium leaks even better than hydrogen, and the bags would have been empty in no time. We couldn't have flown at all with helium."

"But what happened?"

"It was a miracle the Hindenburg flew as far as it did. We should have had the inquiry into why we were so lucky, instead of why the dirigible burned up."

"But..."

"Look, when a big object like that travels around through the skies, it develops big static electricity charges. We tried to reduce the problems by taking various steps, so that lightning bolts would not jump from the ship to the ground, or the towers, or to the crew members on the lines. We also tried to protect the ship in case the lightning bolts did jump, which, of course, we knew they would.

"We tried to make the ship into a giant Faraday Cage. The fabric was thinly coated with metal, so that we would have an unbroken, conducting skin around the whole works, and no electrical spark would come in from outside to start a fire. But that skin was never unbroken. The metallized fabric was not very good, and there were problems with it everywhere. It was merely chance that the problem developed in New Jersey instead of over Berlin. The disaster was inevitable."

"No sabotage, no cloak and dagger?"

"None found by the committee of which I was the secretary with my fountain pen and my trap shut."

"Hydrogen is as dangerous as people fear, then?"

"Who said that? I did not. Hydrogen is very interesting material. We were well aware of its tendency to explode and burn, and we tried very hard to study the matter. A good friend of mine in the company was assigned to investigate the matter very thoroughly.

"The company even constructed a special explosives house for him to work in. You know, it is the sort of light shack they use at dynamite factories. If something explodes in the building, it blows the roof off and away very easily, and the walls fall down outward, so that the workers inside will not be crushed by heavy falling objects. Surprisingly, many people right in the middle of explosions come out uninjured if they are not struck. It is true that their underwear may be blown away during the explosive activity, and they may walk out looking very unusual, but survival is very common.

"My friend worked with the hydrogen diligently for a couple of weeks, trying to make explosions and fires . . . small explosions and fires, but he was unsuccessful. He began to doubt that all the stories about hydrogen were true, and he reported his doubts to our boss.

"He took the boss out to the building to see for himself that the hydrogen would not burn or explode, no matter what he tried.

"He struck a match, and the whole place exploded, of course, walls, roof, everything. Our boss was impressed, but not by the good work that had been done. Yes, they looked unusual when they came back in."

HE COULDN'T MAKE THE HYDROGEN BURN.

"The hydrogen really wouldn't burn?"

"Ah, but you see, hydrogen is not as simple as you think. We know a lot about it that we did not know then. By itself, hydrogen is a good coolant. It does not want to

burn, and cools the thing you are using to start the fire, a
match or a flame. You must have not only a flame, but
the right heating capacitance behind it. The conditions
must be just so."

"And they were just so at Lakehurst."

"They were."

"Otmar, are dirigibles about to come back with new
materials and techniques to become big, slow
freighters?"

"Bah."

ARE DIRIGIBLES ABOUT TO COME BACK?

NOTE: It is difficult to render Dr. Stuetzer's discussion
on paper, partly because the accent he sports gives such
a strong flavor to the talk, and partly because his style is
to sprinkle his profanity with occasional informative
words of English. Strong people quail for a hundred
yards around when he warms up to conversation.
Makes life more interesting in restaurants.

# Who Turned Out the Lights?

Jack was mighty pleased to install his closed circuit television equipment at the laboratory, because he was confident the guys would find it extremely useful. Then they'd buy it, many thousands of dollars worth of stuff. Jack looked forward to the commission.

The application was somewhat exotic. The fellows wanted to see the dials on a number of instruments down in a trench, which was closed off during operation of the equipment. Closed off for good reason. The trench contained a thirty-foot linear accelerator, a prototype of a big machine, a huge machine to be constructed later. What it was, was an atom smasher, and it made the trench more than a little hot when it was operating.

And the television system worked well, let the crews watch the dials on a television screen upstairs. Excellent.

But, gradually, the system dimmed, failed to show what was going on down there. Bah, unreliable equipment. Throw that junk out. Get something that works!

Jack got all his stuff back in a basket with some sharp words. He tested the stuff, isolated the problem component, and looked closer. It was the zoom lens, remotely controlled, at the root of the problem.

The glass in the lens was dark brown. Made of an old beer bottle perhaps, during a careless moment at the lens factory? Well, no. The heavy radiation in the trench

MADE DURING A CARELESS MOMENT AT THE LENS FACTORY?

had turned the glass opaque during the free sample trial period. Two thousand dollars worth of nice glass had been converted to a paperweight.

Jack called attention to his little problem, but was assured by the physicists that nothing of the sort had happened. Faulty equipment, that was his problem. Shame on him.

Want a paperweight?

# It Is To Blush

You've done it, haven't you? Killed the engine at the in-tersection after waving at a friend, glaring at an enemy, catching the cop's eye? Embarrassing.

Imagine being the driver of the pace car at In-dianapolis when it crashed into the stands set up for newspapermen and photographers.

Imagine being the last guy to insist in the newspapers that the Titanic was unsinkable. Imagine being the guy who had to explain to the king why the Wasa did so badly in the water.

THE GUY WHO HAD TO EXPLAIN TO THE KING.

The Wasa? A warship it was, a dandy, big elaborate, and beautiful, the pride of the Scandinavian shipyards, planned as the monarch of the seas. They launched it with considerable ceremony, and it bobbled out across the waves briefly before turning over and sinking like a stone before the impressed audience, some three hundred years ago.

The Wasa has recently served us well, though. Preserved in the cold waters, she has been salvaged, and reassembled. Gives us a clear, useful picture of how not to build or rig a ship of its time. Sic transit, and comes back, Gloria Mundi.

Artist Dick van Bentham spent some years trying to figure out, let alone explain, why he had prepared an elaborate, many panel presentation for the folks at the beer company, and did not discover until the actual presentation that he had left the "l" out of every single representation (and there were many) of the word "Schlitz."

It's traditional, of course, for anarchists and other bombers who are trying to make some conversational point, to blow themselves up with their own rhetoric. Has anybody done a statistical study of the number of deaths caused by folks who throw explosives or merely deposit them at the bank to see who suffers most? Bombers or bankers? Wanna bet? How embarrassing.

Remember the wonderful collection of documentary movies recording the almost-development of the rocket car in Germany? There is the track on which the vehicle is to run. There is the vehicle. There are the officials in their formal garments shaking hands with the driver who is about to take the vehicle for a spin down the track. There are the technicians in protective leather coats. The driver pulls down his goggles, climbs into the car, and settles in. People scurry for cover among the trees. Cut.

There is the vehicle on the track all set to go.

Smoke emerges from the vehicle as the driver throws the switch.

Blooey! There is the explosion as the rocket misfires, throwing large chunks of the vehicle, with driver enclosed, down the track, off the track, over the trees, back into the woods, over the camera. Cut.

There is another vehicle sitting on the track. There are the same officials, the same technicians, the same trees with different leaves. . .and a new driver. They shake hands, he pulls down his goggles, they all run for cover. Cut.

There's the rocket car ready to go. Smoke. BOOOOOM. More flying pieces. Cut.

And, for Goodness' Sake, there's the scene again. Same folks, different vehicle, same trees with no leaves, but lots of snow. . .

Several times over.

It should have been embarrassing, but they apparently just went back to the old drawing board time and again. It was easy enough to get new plans. . .*but what do you suppose they were saying to the drivers?*

We don't have a lot of rocket cars on the road these days.

And then, there was the Kellogg-Briand Pact in the 1920's that ended the arms race and made the world safe. Oh, it didn't? Well, it did a couple of interesting things.

It forced folks to share their plans for battleships, for example. Anybody who built a battleship had to give the plans to other treaty signatories. The British built a battleship, and were unwilling to give out the plans.

Other members of the group fussed and fumed, and spoke reprovingly to the admiralty. Under all that pressure, the British reluctantly disgorged the plans for their battleship.

The Japanese, especially, were interested. (That was back when they copied a lot of things, instead of building better stuff of their own for us to copy.) They copied the battleship, it is said. Launched it, it is said. Fired a practice broadside, it is said.

And turned upside down, and sank.

"Oh, bother," said the admiralty. "We must have given them the wrong plans by mistake. Drat! Dreadfully sorry."

"OH, BOTHER!" SAID THE ADMIRALTY.

Nobody else seems to have built a weapons system according to plans dragged out of the hands of a potential enemy. Funny thing about that. At least we're safe now.

And there was in Chicago a great, big new skyscraper, shiny and impressive, with a grand view of the lake, the park, and (ugh) the rest of Chicago. Handsome.

Early in the game, the tenants began to complain. The ducting for heat and air conditioning also ducted sound hither and yon to unexpected places around the building. Private conversations about the innermost secrets of mobsters were wafted from the lawyer's office to the waiting room of the beauty salon. Talk about gossip! The giggles of the secretary being chased around the executive desk were carried to the employee lunch room.

In all, these effects were disapproved, and were baffled by squads of workers at great expense. The ducts no longer brought news, only air, hot or cold. But wait, there was a bit more.

Somebody ordered an extra trainload of coal with which to heat the building. These things happen. A mountain of black stuff here, a thousand tons there. It adds up. It added up to a pile of coal at the bulding, more than they knew what to do with, lots more. But a resourceful building manager solved the problem.

He had the stuff dumped into an immense empty room under the building that was never used. All that space gone to waste. It was not a handy place to store coal and retrieve it, but it was big enough for a trainload, and with some effort, they stashed away the dusty mountain there.

The room was, of course, the plenum to which all of the air went for the air conditioning and heating system for the skyscraper. No more secrets came through the vents into the offices in this city within the city, but black dust came in quantity, pounds of it, tons of it. The place was one big minstrel show.

Well, it seemed like a good idea at the time.

BLACK DUST IN QUANTITY.

And people *have* built boats, airplanes, trailers, and the like in basements and garages without figuring out in advance how they were going to get these objects up the stairs and out the door.

And there was a driver with a lot to explain in Caracas. You can see the film footage, still. A cameraman was standing on a platform on top of a car in old -fashioned newsreel style while his fellow Yankee driver tooled around the Venezuelan city. The film comes to a sudden end.

So did the cameraman. His driver took him into a low tunnel.

Cameramen get it from all directions. There we were in the mountains above San Bernardino (you don't expect it in Southern California, but those are very high, heavily timbered mountains, where the fellows cut a lot of Douglas Fir), shooting commercials for the famous chain-saw company.

"While the nice man is cutting down the tree," said the director, "you stand around under it with him, recording whatever happens, cracking sounds, hollering timber, whatever it is these guys do." The camera crew, with the director, the agency oaf, and various campfollowers were to set up just beyond the reach of the tree, so they could shoot it falling directly toward them in dramatic style. A longer than average lens would make it look as if it were actually falling on top of them. The magic of movies.

The regional manager for the chainsaw company was there to set things up, look after the saws, and jolly the lumberjack into doing what we wanted.

"These timber beasts are fantastic. Just tell this fellow where you want the tree to fall, just point to the spot, and he'll drop it there within inches. Fantastic. Anything you want, tell him, just tell him."

So they told him where they wanted the tree to fall, and they set up to receive it, with their gaggle of folks all over the area.

I hung around with the lumberjack while he puttered at the base of the tree, preparing to drop it on a dime. I

JUST POINT TO THE SPOT.

could hear the regional manager chattering away en-
thusiastically, burbling about the equipment and the
superhuman skills of the lumberjack.

The lumberjack in turn was gloomily making small
cuts, placing wedges, poking that, tapping this, making
sightings, looking up at the tree. "Funny thing," said he,
"you never know where these things are going to fall. I
don't like that wind. Listen, kid, when things start to get
busy here, get out of the way of the tree. We'll stand here
on this side, and I hope it will fall the other way, but you
really watch, and don't run under the tree. I don't know
what those people over there are planning."

"Just let him know when," said the regional director.

"Sometimes they just break away when you least expect it," said the lumberjack. "Besides, you can't hear
much over the roar of this damn saw. Just hope it waits
'til we drive the wedges."

When at last the monster fell, there was no hearty cry
of "Tiiiimber," just a yelp of fright from the lumberjack,
and some frantic scurrying—at both ends of the tree, for
the things fell thirty feet wide of its mark, amid some

ladies who had gathered around a nice bush, hoping to be photographed somehow. Some shrieking there, but no real damage.

"See?" said the regional manager. "Isn't he wonderful?"

Yep, great.

A month later they dropped the tree right on the camera and killed a couple of the fellows.

Presumably, the regional manager is still bragging up the uncanny control of the guys who use his equipment. If you want to break into show biz, there are fairly frequent openings in certain areas.

You'll enjoy the national atomic museum, too, though the little placards that tell about what you're seeing don't tell quite everything. Well, they wouldn't, would they? There must be some secrets left.

Fascinating museum, really, with the duplicates of the original bomb casings employed at Hiroshima and Nagasaki. Not just copies or models, but additional casings actually made for use at the time. Only chance preserved these casings for the museum instead of the others that were exploded.

There they all are, the artifacts that have been declassified over the decades. (This is a public museum that anybody can tour. There is in addition, we are told, a *classified museum*. Imagine the concept of a hall full of mysterious boxes that are opened only on special occasions to people who have a documented *need to know*. "Here, we can look in this box, but not that one." Charming.) The bombs start big, and grow smaller with time. The hydrogen bombs start *huge*, immense, monstrous, and shrink gradually to something you could cart around in your Honda. All of this is obsolete, or it wouldn't be here, of course.

The exhibit is rendered more interesting by going through it with somebody who was involved with the stuff when it was not obsolete. Little grunts, sighs, groans, and chuckles reveal internal personal stresses that may still not be discussed. From time to time, after a quiet memory search to determine what's fit for public discussion, and what isn't, a little bit of information comes out.

"Look at that," you say. "That's more like what I expect a nice, semi-modern hydrogen bomb to look like."

"Hm, ha," says your companion.

"Gee, I hadn't thought about it before, but that bracket must be bolted to the airplane. You have to hang onto the thing somehow. That must be a good, sturdy piece of steel, and with only two holes in it."

"Gug, grf," says your companion.

"It must be rather heavy, hard to hold when you're making sharp turns in your airplane."

"Uunnnnnh,fmf."

"And look at those holes in the side of the casing, about an inch across. How strange to have holes leading right into the works."

"Well...er...tsk tsk...aaaah, hm," says your companion with more interest, as the wheels grind furiously in his head. "Aah, well, those have a purpose, actually."

"I'll just bet they do. I'm not asking what that purpose is, mind you. Just close-mouthed you, me, and all these security people here. None of us want to hear anything we shouldn't."

"Actually, there's a little we can say about this one, just a little. Nothing all the spies in the world don't already know, but our people don't like to say a lot about it."

"Don't tell me if you shouldn't."

"Um...well...this was a general purpose device, meant to be versatile."

"You mean there's more to it than going Boom on command?"

"Yeah. Maybe you want the thing to go Boom in the air at some particular altitude...or go Boom when it has been parachuted to the surface of a, um, runway or something...or go Boom after it has penetrated twenty feet of concrete and dropped into a tunnel or a submarine pen or something. Maybe you want it to pop after it has reached a certain depth under water."

"Oh."

"Yes, well, it would be a nuisance to carry an assortment of different devices for these different purposes. Better to have one device that can be adapted to different purposes."

"That sounds sensible. What about the holes?"

"The holes, unh, yes, the holes. Well, there are sensors inside the thing, so it knows where it is, in the air, under water, or what."

"So it's automatic."

"Yes, automatic. But there was a problem once, years ago, a problem we don't have today."

"Can you tell me about the problem?"

"I hope so, because I'm going to do it. Are you familiar with mud wasps?"

"Stinging insects that build little mud nests."

"Right, they like to build them inside small holes."

"You don't mean..."

"Sure do. The guys were doing a routine check on a stored device, and they found that mud wasps had built nests inside these nice holes."

"Inside our hydrogen bomb?"

"Well, as I say, inside these nice holes."

MUD WASPS INSIDE THE NICE HOLES.

"More than one?"

"Lots more than one."

"Did this impair the operation of the devices?"

"You can believe there was a real effort to find out. People rushed to look at the devices in the field everywhere. Yes, there were wasps, nests, beetles, flies, bugs of all sorts making themselves at home inside our nuclear weapons, and they were no help."

"Is it fair to say that our defenses were compromised?"

"Ag, gack, fap faw gug, gug, gug."

"Oh. Was there an effort to clean up this matter swiftly?"

"There was a crash engineering effort to design plastic covers for holes in bombs to keep the bugs out, and a fast worldwide distribution of the things."

"And the problem is now years behind us?"

"Yes."

"Good. But the bugs could have beaten us."

"Well, who can say what bugs were in theirs?"

"I see, how reassuring. Oh, what's that over there?"

"Mf zup, ffrl vmoompf."

"Oh."

Now *that's* embarrassing. must have been kidding, wasn't he?

Blush blush blush.

# And For My Next Number . . .

The chapter meeting of the Society of Motion Picture and Television Engineers waited breathlessly (well, some members were sleeping, but quietly) for the promised demonstration of the jam-proof side projector.

Note that slides always jam in the changing mechanism somehow. Some systems jam more often than others, some less. This one promised to work through a compact stack of slides from bottom to top without jamming at all.

The first slide appeared on the screen. Rump-chunk, the second slide appeared on the screen. Rump-chunk, the third slide appeared on the screen. Rump-chunk, the fourth slide pushed halfway in over the third slide, making a sort of mottled montage up on the silver screen.

"Ooops," said the demonstrator nervously, but carefully, so as not to disturb the sleepers.

Rump-chunk, the third slide vanished, leaving the fourth wedged at an angle in the gate. Rattle-Rattle, the image on the screen jumped wildly as the demonstrator shook the projector sternly. Things settled down again. Silence as the angled fourth slide, a picture of a horse in a meadow, shone on the screen framed in spots by brilliant patches of white light leaking around the edges of the slide.

Aha, a mysterious something appeared on the screen with the horse, out of focus. It moved closer, closer,

closer, and revealed itself as the business end of a wooden pencil as focus improved. The pencil stabbed the horse.

Oh, look at that. Those are glass-mounted slides, and the horse has been saved by the invisible protective layer of glass.

Look out, here it comes again.

Tap, tap, smash, smash. As the experts gazed in fascination, the end of the pencil smashed the glass to bits, creating interesting patterns of still another sort on the screen. The world shook as the demonstrator exerted himself in the task of removing slide number four from the jamproof projector.

As the last shards were being dug out of the mechanism, the demonstrator lost his firm grip on the machine, and the brilliant image of destruction flashed across the wall and ceiling, while the projector fell to the floor and smashed the projection bulb.

There was relatively little smoke from the fire, because cool observers pulled the plug and flung a convenient throw rug over the problem before it could spread.

A FAR MORE INTERESTING DEMONSTRATION

The group gave a warm round of applause to the demonstrator as he slunk from the scene with his shattered equipment.

"It was a far more interesting demonstration than the usual demonstration of the jam-proof projector," said one pleased member of the audience. "Usually, they remember to turn off the lamp, and we miss the best part."

# Touch-up

"I didn't really want to work at Los Alamos," said Curly Barr. "I had other plans."

Curly was employed by the Department of the Interior in Albuquerque when the War came along, and attracted his attention. He determined to join the exciting activities, leaving the dull map-making work that was then employing him.

"Ah, no," said his boss on the news of Curly's intention to leave, "we have an important assignment for you right here. You have to stay."

"Well, it's nice to be wanted," said Curly, "But I'm going off to where important things are happening."

"You can't!"

"Like Hell I can't," and Curly went right down, and joined the army.

As a consequence of this forthright act, he was assigned to the Los Alamos atomic bomb development laboratory as a dogface private instead of as a carefree, happy-go-lucky civilian. His participation in exciting events was not actually limited by the assignment. As a photo-instrumentation man, he was one of those shivering on a mountain-top in view of the first atomic test. "There had been a lot of speculation that the shot might actually trigger an uncontrolled chain reaction that would collapse the universe. We were interested to see that it didn't. At least, I don't think it did."

Indeed, as a man who had hunted all over the little populated state of New Mexico, Curly was consulted by the management when it first seemed likely that the bomb might actually work, and it became necessary to find a test site.

"Fine," said Curly. "Get a map, and I'll point out some likely places." Well, they didn't have any good maps, and neither did he. "I'll stop at a gas station and get one," said Curly.

"Oh no. We can't have any of our people asking for maps of the area. Somebody might get suspicious."

"But there's nothing unusual about wanting a map!"

"Don't ask for any maps. Besides, we need something better."

"Well, ask the Department of the Interior. They have good maps. That's what I was working on before you invited me here."

"No, we can't ask Interior."

"Aren't they on our side?"

"Can't risk it. You'll just have to go in, and get the maps we need surreptitiously."

"You mean, steal them?"

"Right."

With classic assurance that if he was caught or killed, the Secretary would deny all knowledge of his activities, Curly crept back into his old office, and swiped some examples of his own work. With those, with a jeep, and with Oppenheimer and Bainbridge, Curly Barr toured New Mexico in search of its most expendable spot. At length, they picked what is now known as the Trinity Site near Alamogordo. One wonders if the gas station maps would have led them elsewhere.

After it was all over, After the War, After we had entered the Atomic Age on tippy-toe, Curly had another relevant assignment. Still at the beck and call of the authorities, he was sent down to Trinity with a basket of explosives and an expert on their use, a young lieutenant.

They went to visit Jumbo.

... SWIPED SOME EXAMPLES OF HIS OWN WORK.

Jumbo was a great big steel bottle that had been fabricated at immense cost in manpower, treasure, and nuisance, back near Chicago or some other mysterious place in the Midwest, at the height of the War. The difficulties of building this thing, and transporting it inconspicuously to the New Mexico desert were extreme. It was a lot of trouble, a *lot* of trouble, but well worth it.

There was a reasonable apprehension that the atomic explosion would not actually occur after the chemical explosion that was supposed to trigger it was set off. The experimenters had visions of spreading small pieces of non-working atomic bomb all over the desert for miles around, and they didn't look forward to collecting all those pieces to assemble another bomb. The plan was to put the whole works inside Jumbo, which could withstand the chemical explosion, and keep the pieces all together in one place in the event of failure of the atomic explosion. Good plan. They demanded, and got, the steel bottle.

Well, maybe not such a good plan. At the last minute, they decided not to use Jumbo. The expensive white elephant was left over at the side of the test site, out of the way. Things worked out well enough, because the

atomic explosion was achieved, and Jumbo wasn't actually needed. Splendid. Still, there it remained as a con-
tinuous reproach to the people who had required all that
money to be spent on it, while other important things
were ignored.

So Curly and the nice man with the explosives arrived
on the scene. "We climbed into the bottle," said Curly,
"and the lieutenant placed some charges around the inside. I didn't know why we were doing this, and I was
impressed by the amount of material he was planning to
blow." They climbed back out, and ran the wires off
some distance from the bottle.

The lieutenant prepared to set off the blast. "Wait,"
said Curly, "we put quite a lot of stuff in that bottle.
Don't you want to get farther away from it before you set
it off?"

"Nothing to worry about," said the man. "That's just a
little firecracker we've got in there. It won't do anything
to that jug but char the insides a little."

"Do you mind waiting until I go over and lie down in
that ditch?"

The man didn't mind.

When he set off the charges, Curly reported, the neck
of the bottle was blown clear off. It flew through the air,
past the ditch in which the uneasy Curly was lying. The
noise was stunning, and the cloud of smoke and debris
entirely satisfying.

"You never saw an explosives expert so embarrassed,
but I was glad that neither of us had been hurt. I guess
we just had different points of view on the matter. We
went away and left it all there; I never did find out why
we had done it at all . . . but I have my suspicions. I think
General Groves got to thinking about how many questions there would be from reporters who wondered
what that big steel thing was near the shot site. He probably figured it would be easier to explain if the thing had
obviously been used for containing an explosion. The effect was obvious, all right, but the containment wasn't

what they were hoping for. I think the flying chunk was picked up, and put on display over in Socorro."

"Humbug," cries the public relations group now responsible for explaining things at the atomic bomb works, "the history of Jumbo is well known, and does not include any incident like that. It is damaged, all right, the ends are blown out of it, because it was used in a series of explosive tests. So much for Mr. Barr's veracity!"

In July 1979, a crane moved the carcass of Jumbo from the brush at some distance from the Trinity Site to a spot right next to the circle of fused glass that marks the beginning of our era. Once a year a caravan of visitors is escorted to the scene. It will be easier for them now to admire Jumbo.

This removal of the steel jug from its accustomed resting place prompted a call to Curly. "They may have done something else to it after we blew the neck off," said he with many a chortle. "If you want some more information to check on, I'll get it, and give you a call back. I'll call you back in a few days."

And then Curly up and died without calling. Sometimes his plans just didn't work out.

# Short Take-off and Landing

Well sure, now that they sometimes work, helicopters are very convenient. They can land on your roof, and take off again from there, even if you are surrounded by tall trees and buildings. If this is your idea of a good thing, the capability makes you happy. But helicopters are expensive and fussy.

That business about the ground effect that people discovered and solved in the early helicopter days is still troublesome, adding mightily to the cost of the aircraft. The blades change their pitch as they turn, there are swash plates to deal with, and expensive, heavy gear boxes. The problems are all borne with the aid of money and iron nerve, but one wishes for something better.

Many a thoughtful aeronautical innovator has turned his attention from helicopters to autogiros. An autogiro is a more-or-less conventional airplane with a rotating wing that makes it look like a helicopter. No power to those blades on the giro; the plane sports a standard propeller to give the craft forward motion, so the wings have lift.

But the rotating wing is nice in its way. It gives a *lot* of lift, so the plane can travel at rather low speed, can take off with a very short run, and will not drop like a brick onto the freeway if engine power fails. The giro just mushes in, almost vertically.

There lived in Ocala, Florida, a fertilizer magnate who realized that the autogiro could be crossed with the helicopter to provide in a single kludge the better features of both. Notably, the craft could take off vertically.

The innovator reasoned that a helicopter gearbox was complex, heavy, and expensive, chiefly because it had to work all the time. Under very limited conditions, it could be simple, light, and cheap. Not bad thinking.

(In later years, this same chap gave a dairy, complete with cows, milk, and equipment to an Indian tribe to improve their health and their economy. Cats, rats, bats, ferrets, weasels, polar bears, and *Caucasian* human beings retain their infantile tolerance for lactose, the natural sugar in all milk. Other mammals, including Indians from ancient and honorable Mongol stock quit drinking milk early in life, most of them, because it makes them sick, owing to the lack of lactase. What Indians tend to do with the milk provided for their well being is get rid of it. One assumes that the cows were tasty. No milk is for sale from that firm at the moment.)

NO MILK IS FOR SALE FROM THAT FIRM.

So he built an autogiro that put power to the rotor *temporarily*, only  while the craft was taking off. Nothing fancy, the gears just made the rotor turn until the vehicle climbed high enough to clear the surrounding obstacles. Then the pilot would pull power from the rotor, throw it to the conventional prop, and fly away in the autogiro. The little pause between powered rotor and powered prop gave the pilot a thrill at each take-off, but flying is a dicey game at best, and the added fright was considered no great drawback.

Word of this marvelous machine circulated in a limited way while the developers solved one problem after another, working toward official approval, and marketing. Skeptics abounded, as ever. The sages said it wouldn't work.

When the big public presentation finally came along, it was a major event, ballyhooed vigorously, attracting newspeople with cameras from far and wide.

The introductory remarks to the throng did not drive the listeners all away, and the cameras were rolling as the pilot climbed in, ran through his quaint rituals, fired up the engine, and prepared for takeoff.

He put the power to the rotor, which increased its speed at a deliberate, but satisfying rate until it could lift the plane. Then the craft lightly left the ground, up, up, up, until the pilot judged the time appropriate to switch from lift to push. He threw the lever.

The national television audience had a great view of this procedure on the evening news. The machine flipped over on its side, and the rotor assumed the role of a huge wheel, rolling along the grass, a bit lopsided, because of the airplane, pilot, motor, and all that fastened to its hub. Wham, wham, wham! A remarkable distance. The crowd followed, afoot, until the action stopped.

A fine demonstration, one of the best. Well worth seeing. If you missed that one, you may have a long wait before the girocopter is displayed with such flair again. You may want to stand back a little from the center of the action.

# So Near, and Yet . . .

Friday night, almost five o'clock.

The carpenters were finishing the last little task of the day, had already been paid, and were looking forward to a fine weekend, financed by cashing of the paychecks.

The last task was touchy, like many. It involved putting a piece of Formica down on a counter top. That's a nerve-wracking chore, because the technique is to slather the wooden counter-top with a powerful cement, and let it dry. Then you slather the bottom of the Formica with the cement, and let it dry.

When these two surfaces come in contact, they *grab* and hold. Forever. The wood will break away and the Formica crumble to powder before that stickum releases. Wonderful stuff.

However, it put a premium on careful placement of the Formica. There's no second chance. If you make a false move, and touch the surfaces together awkwardly, the jig is up. You rebuild the whole thing from scratch. Really, a couple of workers accustomed to doing this as a team almost never miss. There's a rhythm to it. Hup, hoop, snap...there! There's a beautiful finality to the process.

So they hupped, hooped, and snapped. As the eternal union between the surfaces was made, one man's

A BEAUTIFUL FINALITY

paycheck fluttered gracefully from his pocket, and slipped between the parts. There!

Who's that muttering and bumbling in the darkness over at the construction site?

# The Trike

After the war, some people felt that improvements and changes could be made in automobiles. Time for new cars. The Crosley reached the market suddenly. It was an interesting little cage in which the driver hunched over the wheel behind a surplus landing craft engine. People kept fleets of Crosleys so they could cannibalize parts from several to keep one running. Transportation and a hobby all in one.

There was the ill-fated Tucker, a saga in itself. Poor old Tucker himself was convicted of bad behavior in the long run, after stretching himself to the point of desperation and craziness to get his new vehicle manufactured and established over the implacable resitance of those who ruled Detroit. Things didn't work out well for this innovator.

The Henry J, Mr. Kaiser's marvel, was among us for a few years, a small, American-made car that has some nostalgic appeal in gas-short times. The Kaiser-Frasers came and went more quickly.

And there was a three-wheeler.

Really, a highway automobile with three wheels, a rounded, bulbous rolling thing. A three hundred pound man in San Mateo, California drove one of the few that were sold to the public. Yes, the vehicle did sag dramatically to the left, distracting bemused drivers in the cars following for some years.

Only a few sold? Didn't the car have what people wanted, novelty, economy, postwar styling, promise for the future, pizzaz? Yes, it had those things in some measure, but it also had only three wheels, and that made people nervous. "Unstable," was the common feeling. "That thing will tip over like a kid's tricycle if it has half a chance."

Not so, insisted the proud and distressed developer. He would show that it was as stable as Gibraltar, firmly and forever planted on the ground.

"I'll prove it," said he. "Those of you who work in Chicago's Loop are invited to Soldier's Field at noon of a workday. Bring you lunch, sit in the bleachers, and watch the show."

People did that. Scads of them carried brown paper bags over to the famous athletic field, and sat there, munching their baloney while the demonstration began.

A few words, some introductions, a testimonial, then the demonstration. The driver climbed into the three-wheeler, sped down the track before the stands, whipped into the first turn, and rolled over.

"Uh-huh. Finish your sandwich, Charlie, and let's get back to the office."

Three-wheeled cars haven't caught on, still.

A TESTIMONIAL, THEN THE DEMONSTRATION.

# Anybody Seen an Oasis Nearby?

Cinerama was spectacular beyond adequate description when it was first introduced back in the early fifties. The first really big wide-screen movie process, Cinerama, used three cameras with three strips of film to record a single panoramic view. Then three projectors were employed to throw that panoramic image on one big screen. Wow. Lowell Thomas appeared in the introductory film. The sequence for introduction at the beginning was shot with a regular old camera, and seemed a bit disappointing to the crowds in the thronged theaters. As Thomas finished his presentation, though, the curtains at the sides of the center screen pulled back, and the small image spread and spread to fill the whole front of the theatre with magnificent, frightening images that thrilled viewers just all to pieces. In its time, compared with what had come before, Cinerama was marvelous.

It had a problem or two.

It was terribly difficult to match the color in the three separate pieces of film running through the projectors. No matter what the technicians did, no matter how well they fitted those pictures together, they still looked like three separate pictures. More, the images jittered a bit on the screen, because the projector mechanisms are not perfect,and the three images in slightly different colors did not match perfectly at the edges. All projected movie images jitter, but the effect was exaggerated when the three jittered in different ways at the same time. This made for a certain amount of headache and nausea, but people didn't mind too much.

A producer name of Mike Todd perceived that huge images were boffo at the box office, and that they would be even better if somebody solved the three-image problem.

Nothing was simpler, he reasoned. One need only use a bigger piece of film for each image of a movie, to allow sufficient resolution, and use a lens that would record an undistorted, ultra-wide-angle picture on that big piece of film. Quit fooling around! Do it right!

Mike Todd was solid brass, a daring and exciting promoter in show business whose mad schemes paid off in marvelous entertainment, and often in large sums of money. Todd was a risk-taker on a gigantic scale. Typical Todd story: He was on hard times, without cash for any project, but he maintained a huge suite of offices on several floors of a downtown New York building. A friend remarked that he should economize by getting rid of all that overhead cost.

"Look," Todd is reported to have said, "I owe people about four million dollars. You want me to give up cigars?"

He hustled together a company whose charter it was to produce the camera and projection system that would throw a veritable football field-sized image on a screen without the motley color variation and the clashing jitters.

American Optical Company was among the members of the new firm, called TODD AO. Somebody had an approach to doing the job, and TODD AO acquired the rights to the process, digging into the job with a will. Somehow, most of the actual work fell on American Optical. The work consumed most of their attention and cash for some years.

The work is not remembered all that clearly, these twenty-five and some years later, and many of the survivors prefer to forget the whole thing, but here is a fuzzy, jittery, variegated, Cinerama-style picture of TODD AO. Bits and pieces.

The necessary camera lens was a bit special. The design called for eleven elements in the lens, eleven separate pieces of glass, all shaped just so, all of certain refractive indices, all spaced just so. The last element was aspheric.

If you take a piece of glass, or anything, drop it in a bag of grit, and jostle it around, it will come out round. The longer you justle, the rounder it gets, because the hard little particles keep knocking off corners until there aren't any. Whatever it is gets rounder and rounder. There are other considerations, but basically, making a *spherical* lens is a predictable and reliable process. Making an aspherical lens is a trying experience. Only thirty-nine out of forty attempts at making high precision spherical lenses fail (the rejects are good enough for rework or for lower quality applications), while the rejection rate on aspherics is extremely high and the rejects are good for very little.

Just in passing, an aspheric requires you first to make a Green Block. Who knows where the name came from- . . . maybe the first ones were made of something green, or maybe Joe Green invented them or something. Anyway, a Green Block is a hunk of metal in which you have machined a hollow approximately the shape of the lens you want.

What you do with the Green Block is drop it – no, not from a foot, just a very little way, on a piece of glass that has been chipped off to a very approximate size and shape of your lens.

This also chips off the corners. You repeat the process, on and on, until the block and the glass have both been worn and smoothed closer to what you had in mind. Then there are finishing processes a little less peculiar. If you feel that this is a mighty crude way to go about making lenses, you are right. If you have some better ideas that will actually work, there are folks who would like to hear from you. They don't want to hear about ideas that don't work already, thank you.

So, there was an aspheric last element in the TODD AO camera lens. The *front* element was spherical, all right, but it was concave, about one eighth of an inch thick in the center, an inch thick at the edges, and overall, bowed. More, the glass needed for this had a somewhat unusual index of refraction, and a diligent search revealed that only the National Bureau of Standards actually possessed chunks of this glass big enough for the purpose. NBS made the chunks available. Oh, yes, the lens was eight and a half inches in diameter.

Those were the first and last lenses. The other nine elements were special in their own ways. Art, not science, was the key to development of this monstrosity. AO put its finest gnomes on the project, and tried to stay out of their hair.

The magical individual assigned to create that front lens from the rare glass applied himself steadfastly to the task, and after some months, had it finished. A marvel. It was ready.

He took it gently off the machine, and put it down with equal care on the bench. He looked up. He heard a ping. He did not look down. He went home and composed himself, then called the plant to inquire about the lens element on his bench. Oh that? Gee, it's cracked.

He started over. . .and the only two appropriate pieces of glass remaining in the world survived the process to make excellent lenses.

The completed assembly – there were, and presumably *are*, two of them – was huge. It weighed many pounds, was worth all the tea in China, and dominated the lives of the people who dealt with it. The lens was mounted on its own base, and the camera mechanism was a mere appendage. The crown jewels never had it so good.

The projection lens was less exacting optically, but the projection system had its own problems. The problems stemmed fundamentally from a basic fact: All of the

THE CAMERA MECHANISM WAS A MERE APPENDAGE.

light reaching the screen comes from a single source. If the source is a one hundred watt bulb, the brightness of the image on the screen depends on the efficiency of the projection system in catching the light from that bulb and pumping it through the film, the amount of that light absorbed by the film and the other optical elements, and the size of the screen. If you spread those hundred watts over a certain area, the image has a certain level of brightness. If you spread that same amount of light over a larger area, the screen seems dimmer.

The TODD AO system was designed to spread the available light over a huge area, and the brightness has to be high. The film itself absorbed about half of the available light on the average. The projector needed about a four thousand watt arc to produce enough light. It could also roast an ox pretty fast with the heat. It was no simple matter to avoid vaporizing the film when it was exposed to this great energy.

Indeed, at the first projection attempt, the projection lens elements absorbed so much energy that the lenses shattered.

In another attempt, the glass and the aluminum in the projection lens both melted, and ran in a puddle in the bottom of the box housing them. An observer who ar-

rived on the scene while things were still glowing commented: "It was terribly impressive. People were standing around, staring into that puddle and saying over and
over, 'Who would have thought it would be that hot?'"

... STARING INTO THAT PUDDLE.

They addressed the problem in various ways. The projectors eventually used in theaters were quite complex.
For example, the lens elements were coated with trans-
parent resistive material. The electricity was switched
on as a first step, and the lenses were heated by these
resistors almost to the point of incandescence. This
reduced the shock when the arc was struck, and
diminished the probability of exploding lenses.

There was some little problem in getting the film in
focus on both the edges of the huge screen, and the middle of the huge screen. The lens simply couldn't focus
everything recorded on the flat piece of film onto the
somewhat curved screen. Solution—curve the film
while it is in the gate with the light pouring through it.
This was accomplished by directing a powerful jet of air,
a hurricane of air, into the middle of the frame right in
the gate. The blast deformed the film just enough so that
everything was in focus on the screen at the same time.
The wind also had the attractive side effect of cooling
things just a bit.

Do you have the impression that this was a kludge, that the engineering was a collection of ideas that just barely worked, all strung together, and that a lot of lucky things had to work at the same time in projection rooms all over the country? You are correct.

And did they work?

They worked beautifully, magnificently. The system was fully gratifying. Todd's vision was brought to full reality in a way that delighted and uplifted millions of people.

American Optical was proud of its accomplishments as well. The rumor circulated in the company that the project caused them a loss of four and a half million dollars. AO looked upon Todd as part of their problem, not as part of their solution to financial worries.

It wasn't just the difficult technology; they'd bargained for that, taken their chances with a potential for big returns. They hadn't meant to get quite so far into show business with a crazy-mad promoter. The incidental expenses were surprising.

Came time to test the system.

"Great," said the AO technicians, "we'll go over to the park in Buffalo."

"The park? In Buffalo? New York?"

"Yes, well, this is a wide angle lens we have made, and we really should take it outside for a real test."

"Of course outside. This is a very wide-angle lens. We need a very wide-angle scene to try it on."

"Yes, the park."

"Not the park. What's the widest-angle thing you can think of?"

"Unh . . . Niagara Falls?"

"No no."

"No?"

"The desert."

"Not really. The park is just as wide."

"You're talking about technology. I'm talking about hearts and souls and money and faith and the investors.

A picture of a park is a picture of a park. A picture of a desert is magic. We need magic."

"We need a test of a lens. We could do it in the lab."

"We need romance. We're going to the desert."

"What desert?"

"A wide-angle desert, with dunes, vista, expanse. We'll find one."

They found one, way out west.

They loaded up everybody and everything, and flew off to the desert. Set up the lens with camera attached, and peered through the view finder. It was not satisfactory.

"Empty, ain't it? You can't tell how big it really is, because there's nothing in it."

"Right, let's go back to the park. It has trees."

"Naw. The desert is the right place; it just needs one thing. What does it need?"

"Trees?"

"No, what's in every desert you ever saw?"

"I never saw a desert, only this one."

"In pictures."

"Sand?"

"Camels."

"Let's go to the park."

"Camels, get camels, lots of camels, a hundred."

"I can't get a hundred camels."

"Call your office."

"They don't have camels."

"No, but get them working on it."

"They don't know anything about camels either."

"They have lots of people and lots of phones. They can find camels."

"But the money, and the time."

"We'll wait."

"But . . ."

"TODD AO will pay."

"But . . ."

"Am I not authorized to commit the company?"

"Sure, but..."

"Find the camels."

They found camels, a whole lot of them. Almost all came from zoos in various cities around the country that were glad to rent the cranky critters out for a fee.

These camels had spent their lives in the quiet calm of tree shaded parks, watered and fed and admired. They had not been carrying heavy burdens over blazing sands. Their feet were tender. The moviemakers now had a desert and camels, but the animals just milled around, trying to find some way to keep all four feet off the ground at once. They made a sorry picture.

TRYING TO KEEP ALL FOUR FEET OFF THE GROUND.

Resisting all entreaties to do something sensible, Todd sought a way to make the most of his wide-angle desert and camels.

"Camels must get sore feet sometimes."

"Sure, they have sore feet now."

"They must be able to protect those feet."

"Yeah, they try to lie down under a tree with their feet in the air."

"No, my boy. Shoes; I'm talking about shoes."

"Camel shoes?"

"Get them, we need four hundred."

"The time, the expense! We've already been here for weeks."

The offices in Buffalo began to bustle once again as all free hands were turned to the search for camel shoes. Anything to make the ordeal come to an end. Nobody knew what the total U.S. supply of camel shoes might be, if such a product existed at all, but no effort was too great to make.

In fact, they found camel shoes, even an adequate supply. One hitch. They were purple.

Todd was satisfied. He had something dramatic to work with, something around which to build a show for the backers, past and future. A fellow couldn't really go wrong with the widest-angle lens in the world, a nice wide-angle desert, and a wide-angle line of camels in gorgeous purple shoes, toiling across the dunes in a proper caravan.

His partners in TODD AO, good, practical people, were at their wit's end, dragged into one expensive crisis after another, bound for financial ruin. They longed to be rid of this man, to drive him away, leaving them with the hardware that had cost so much. And they managed it.

One of the AO people came in beaming. "We've done it," he said, "forced him out at last, forced him out." TODD AO kept the name, but Todd was out.

The mechanism for forcing him to go?

They arranged to give him eight million dollars.

And that certainly taught him a lesson, Ollie. Hmph!

Todd went on to produce *Around the World in Eighty Days*, with a financial scare every few minutes. It became a classic, and its story has been told repeatedly. It made money, too.

Todd's gone, killed in a plane crash now long ago, but the stories about him, some of them possibly even true, linger on in cheery memory.

Some of the AO folks remember him ever so well.

... FORCED HIM OUT AT LAST.

# Jaws

Paul brought his lunch in a brown bag every day. He'd fold himself into the sofa in the waiting room, pull out a book, pull out his sandwich, and feed his mind while he fed his face. The book had his greater attention.

One day he bit off a piece of his sandwich, chewed it abstractedly while reading, gagged it down, and looked up from the page to glance curiously at the sandwich for a moment. It wasn't doing anything special, so he looked back at the book while taking another bite.

That bite wasn't easy, great effort was required to tear a chunk out of the sandwich. Paul put the book on his knee while he lifted the top slice of bread, and peered with concern at the mayonnaise, lettuce, and salami on the bottom slice of bread. Still nothing of special note.

He took another bite with equal difficulty. After he chewed it some, and swallowed, he set his reading aside firmly. He set the sandwich on the table beside him, and disassembled it in workmanlike fashion, laying the elements out side by side. Nothing untoward.

There they lay, crying for scientific examination.

He turned over the top bread. Nothing.

He turned over the leaf of lettuce. Nothing.

He examined the mayonnaise, by now spread conveniently on the table top. Nothing.

He peered at the slice of meat. Peered closer. Finally picked up the piece of salami, and turned it over.

The other side was white.

He turned it again. One side was still the finest looking piece of salami ever offered to a cranky man in a sandwich. Yes, but the other side was indisputably stark white. A fast-growing mold, perhaps?

He picked up the salami, and studied it more intently, turning it round and round.

"Oh," he said at last, and swept all the pieces into the wastebasket. He sighed, and settled to read, feeding body and soul alike on literature.

A study of the remnants revealed the rest of the details to the now-eager crowd of onlookers. On one side of that salami appeared salami. On the other side, merely the grain of the white piece of cardboard that is the end-piece in a package of salami. The good-looking cold-cut was really a handsome, full color, printed representation of salami.

A STUDY OF THE REMNANTS.

Paul had been eating, not a salami sandwich, but a picture-of-salami sandwich created by his sleepy wife on the family lunch assembly line that morning.

"Didn't *taste* any different," said Paul.

# Secret Weapons

The U.S. engineers perspired over their task, rapid development of several identical, extraordinarily complex machines. The work was finished on time, and the machines were flown away to be parachuted into various parts of Germany. It turned out that all of the devices were discovered by the Germans.

Then the German engineers perspired, throwing heavy manpower and resources into examination of these new weapons. What were they for? They were designed to occupy a large number of German engineers; that's what. And they did.

DESIGNED TO OCCUPY GERMAN ENGINEERS.

There was a superstition in those ancient times that German radar could be confused, would fail to identify their targets clearly, if bombers' crews filled the air with fluttering bits of metal chaff.

Consequently, people spent large amounts of energy, cutting tin cans to bits so that fliers could scatter them into the sky over the Fatherland.

"Bah," said Dr. Stuetzer, "the chaff did not confuse the radar at all, but it certainly did confuse our people. We could not imagine why anybody would throw that stuff out of airplanes, unless it was an effort at germ warfare. We thought perhaps the metal was coated with infectious material, and that the sharp edges were designed to create cuts that would encourage rapid spread of the infection. It never occurred to us that it had anything to do with radar."

# Whoa

An airplane propeller drags the ship forward through the air as it turns. If you turned the propeller the other way, would it push the plane backward?

Yes.

But that's impractical, even assuming that you want to go backward, because it's inconvenient to kludge together all the gears and mechanism to reverse the spin on a prop.

It is practical, however, to reverse the pitch of the prop blades, by turning them in the hub, so that even while the prop is turning in the same direction, it may either pull or push, depending on the orientation of the blade.

And that is a valuable capability, because the desirable *bite* of a propeller in the air varies with a number of factors, and it's efficient to change the pitch appropriately. Too, the pilot does often want to push back on the plane, instead of moving forward. When you have landed, and are rolling down the runway, it's nice to be able to slow down by reversing the prop pitch, instead of just applying the brakes in the wheels.

The reversing prop was developed in the thirties, and was not widely used before the war. (Surely Leonardo and others up through the years had experimented with the idea, but it was rendered in practical form only late in the game.)

A reversing-pitch system was installed on a Thunderbolt fighter plane, it is said. The Thunderbolt was a big plane, as big as the DC-3, with a huge single engine in the nose.

The pilot who first flew the monster with the reversing prop did well with it until it came time to land. Landing aircraft is always a touchy job, somehow, probably because getting back onto the ground safely is looked upon subconsciously as the single most important part of any flight. It weighs on your thoughts when it comes time to land.

This chap got a bit muddled with the extra control, the one that lets him change the pitch of his prop. He noticed that he was not traveling fast enough, and he gave the ship a bit of gas. That still didn't speed him up satisfactorily, but he remembered that he had the variable pitch prop under his command, and he adjusted it to hasten his approach a little. It didn't help.

Gradually, he increased the engine speed, while adjusting the pitch, and could not correct his situation. He grew more tense as the ground approached, and made more decisive moves. As he reached the very tip of the runway, it seemed to him that he was going completely out of control, so he gunned the engine with full throttle, and adjusted the prop to the limits of its range.

Sure, he was turning the prop the wrong way.

Easy for us to know, but he was under pressure.

The effect was that the aircraft came to a dead stop in midair with a colossal roar of its immense engine, and dropped the last ninety feet straight down, attracting the attention of everybody for miles around.

Flat as a pancake. The wheels came up through the wings and the engine tore itself up as the prop bit into the pavement.

No injury to the pilot, just an uncommonly dramatic landing.

... WITH FULL THROTTLE.

# If At First . . .

An airplane blew up on the ground, and there was some official curiosity as to the cause. Tracking things back to the beginning, the Air Force people found this chain of events.

First, industrial gases like Oxygen, $CO_2$, Nitrogen, and Hydrogen are clearly marked according to strong conventions. Oxygen is to be put up only in a green bottle, for example, hydrogen only in red. The bottles are not only painted in identifying colors, but are marked with tags of matching color, so there is a check at frequent intervals on the contents of any bottle in use, because people are interested in how much it holds, how long it has lasted, and all that, and they look at the tag for the information.

The commercial firm that supplied gases to these airplanes followed the conventions rigidly.

One afternoon, a workman put a single red bottle of hydrogen on a truck full of green bottles of oxygen. The red bottle stuck out like a sore thumb. Unluckily, someone had tied a green tag to this red bottle. Tag and bottle didn't match. The bottle color said hydrogen. The tag color said oxygen. The bottle actually contained hydrogen.

The bottles were all delivered to the base, and checked in, formally accepted. They were stored in a warehouse full of green oxygen bottles. The one red bottle was an attention-compelling anomaly among the green bottles.

The time came to distribute oxygen bottles to the planes, and a couple of fellows with a jeep picked up the green-tagged red bottle among the green-tagged green bottles. They hauled the red bottle to an airplane and replaced the green oxygen bottle in the plane with the red bottle of hydrogen. Then they tried to connect the red bottle to the plane's oxygen system. It wasn't easy.

For one thing, the threads on the red bottle were left-handed, rather than right-handed. This precaution was carefully planned to prevent accidental hookup of hydrogen bottles to oxygen systems. No matter, they overpowered the resisting connector with a bigger wrench, and made the hookup.

A BIGGER WRENCH

For another thing, the hydrogen leaking from the connector caught fire twice when sparks from the slipping wrench struck the flow. The crew alertly smothered the flames both times, and left the hydrogen tank securely integrated with the oxygen system on the plane when they left. A job well done.

After a bit, all of the connected oxygen tanks on the plane exploded, completely destroying the bomber.

The authorities were especially curious about the possibility of sabotage to this valuable warplane. Indeed, the guy who put the green tag on the red bottle was never identified.

But the conclusion was that the whole thing was an accident. No saboteur could have been so wildly optimistic as to think he could destroy an airplane this way.

SO WILDLY OPTIMISTIC

# Temper, Temper

Tempered glass is not uncommon now. Your glasses may be tempered, so you can drop them on hard floors, face a hail of gravel with confidence, and the like. Tempered glass was not always common, and a chap who had a piece of it in the early fifties made great use of it as an item of conversation and wonder.

He'd toss it on the floor, tap it on fireplace bricks, and generally revel in making people nervous about having broken glass in their soup.

An acquaintance of his was doing an educational television show once a week, explaining science to people who couldn't find anything better to watch. Tempered glass was just his meat, and the television sage eagerly borrowed the hunk of glass.

When he came on the air live, he said a few words about the glass, held it up next to his ear, tapped it with a pencil. . .and the glass instantly turned to powder, drifting across the studio in a sorry cloud.

The sage was struck dumb. He stammered in confusion, and spent the rest of his time trying to explain what might have happened. For years he nursed the suspicion that he'd been set up. His dreams are filled with images of himself explaining to a huge audience that he has a piece of unbreakable glass, and then the glass breaks when he looks at it hard. Fate has singled him out for torment.

TAPPED IT WITH A PENCIL.

Well, no. Glass does that, especially thick pieces that have a chance to build internal stresses. When our laboratory crew was putting together a little vacuum system, and needed a thick, round piece of glass with a hole in it for the top of the vacuum pot, somebody picked up an old porthole window at a surplus place. Just the thing, and cheap.

The people at the place that makes holes in glass to specification called the next day with a report. "Your porthole exploded." It wasn't all that hard to find another suitable piece of glass, but it took a long while to explain to the business manager, the vice-president of research, and ultimately the board of directors why they had purchased a porthole in the first place, let alone how it could have exploded.

Internal stresses, that's why. Stresses relieved by a very fine scratch at the surface, or a tap at some critical point with a pencil.

One of the great atomic works had a four-inch thick, leaded glass window through which workers could peer in safety at events in the radioactive area beyond a wall.

A janitor reached up with a dusting cloth one evening, and dragged a tiny particle across the glass, creating stress risers. All that energy soaked up from the heavy radiation over the years found a place to go. Their porthole exploded.

That janitor apologized. It's embarrassing to break a window.

THEIR PORTHOLE EXPLODED.

# The Tally

There was a chap working for the Air Corps as a pilot during World War II who achieved a notable distinction without striving for it. He was a pilot, a civilian under contract, who, by a peculiar set of circumstances, was authorized to fly military aircraft.

He was warming up the engines on a B-17, the fabled Flying Fortress, last of the big bombers to use a tail wheel while sitting on the ground like a DC-3, instead of using the now standard tricycle landing gear of big aircraft. As he waited for the temperatures to rise, he toyed idly with the many switches on the panel, trying this and that.

He tried the switch that caused the landing gear to retract. Wise designers had foreseen this sort of activity, and prepared for it. The wheels would not retract while the plane sat on the ground. Safe.

Well, almost safe.

The whirring props created just enough lift with the air flowing over the wings, so that the craft was essentially weightless. The safety mechanism thought the B-17 was flying, and did raise the wheels.

There was a deal of crunching, and a deal of damage. The plane was knocked out of service for a spell. Pity, but understandable in a way, and the Air Corps needed pilots.

On another occasion, this pilot was driving one airplane on the ground, and managed to run into another airplane on the ground, causing extensive damage that knocked both aircraft out of service for an extended period of time, but accidents do happen. . . and the Air Corps needed pilots.

During a test flight, this pilot discovered difficulties in operation of the aircraft that forced him to bail out, while the plane crashed, totally destroyed. Well, that's what test flights are all about, aren't they? And the Air Corps needed pilots.

THAT'S WHAT TEST FLIGHTS ARE ALL ABOUT.

Late in the war there was an outbreak of trouble with combat aircraft. In one eighteen day period, twenty one planes went down for no clear reason, most war-weary P-38's. Profound worry set in, and a massive test program was launched, during which all critical parts on all U.S. aircraft were subjected to exacting inspection.

One hundred and fifty airplanes were found not just to be tired, but actually to have cracked wing spars. Compared with this effort and this discovery, the recent stir about engine mounts on the DC-10 seems not so impressive.

A policy decision was made to survey these aircraft, rather than fix them. (*Survey* is a now evidently obsolete military term meaning *throw away*.) They decided to throw the planes away instead of messing with them.

You don't just leave equipment like this out for the trash man, though. You take it to some central place where people can watch it rot under appropriate conditions. One way to move the planes was to take them apart, load the pieces on ground vehicles, and carry them at great expense to the field where they would be stored. Ridiculous.

They were to fly to the field. No big risk, really; a gentle flight under favorable, non-combat, non-stress conditions. Should be a piece of cake. Our man was one chosen to ferry these wrecks to the junkyard. He couldn't go wrong.

Well, he could, actually.

As soon as he got off the ground with an airplane about which he was not much worried, he began to try exercises like snap rolls that really give a plane a workout.

Sure enough, a wing fell off.

He bailed out.

Well, it was going to the junkyard, anyway, wasn't it? And nobody had specifically forbidden him to do snap rolls. The Air Corps needed pilots.

And this one was special. He is the only U.S. pilot known to have destroyed five airplanes, all in California.

He was an Ace.

ALL IN CALIFORNIA

# You're Not Covered For That

So they sent the two thousand dollars to the company that very day, in spite of the strain on finances, and had the computer terminal shipped out promptly to Louisiana, where it arrived smashed to pieces. The important sales presentation that depended on the terminal was scheduled for the following week.

"Well," said the carrier, "we can probably get an inspector out there within the next month."

"No," said the manufacturer, "the terminal was yours as soon as we delivered it to the carrier. Why don't you just buy another for your presentation, and maybe we can make some deal to take one back later? Oh, sure, we'd need the two G's cash for it."

"No," said the insurance man, "if the airplane had crashed with the terminal, or if a meteorite had fallen on it, or if the delivery truck had fallen from a bridge, or if there had been a fire at the distribution warehouse, we'd be able to pick that up, but we just don't cover anything that's likely to happen under that expensive policy. You'll have to settle it with the carrier..."

Sigh.

The movie on safety called for a careless motorboat steersman, paying too much attention to a water skier behind him, to crash into a swimming raft in the lake. It was necessary to stage a real crash.

IF A METEORITE HAD FALLEN ON IT...

The fuel line was loosened at the motor. The director himself was to steer the speeding boat to the raft, yank the line away from the motor, and slide overboard. The boat would run long enough to crash, but the shortage of fuel from the detached line would stop it before it went anywhere.

In his pride and excitement, he revved the boat up to full speed, and slipped over the side, but forgot to pull the fuel line all the way free of the engine. A big, powerful speedboat was now raging about the small lake without a pilot.

It smashed the raft to kindling, making a very nice picture, and sped on toward a line of moored sailboats, but fell into a left turn before reaching them, and missed. Instead, the boat make huge loops around the lake, weaving among the swimmers, grabbing the lines of fishermen, terrorizing folks who had rented rowboats for an hour's galley labor in the hot sun. But no damage. Missed them all.

At length, the boat was diverted again by its own giant wake, and it headed straight for the shore, missed a pier, missed another raft, and made a magnificent attempt to kill a nice man who was sitting on his cottage porch two hundred feet from the shore. The propeller dug an interesting trench in the man's lawn before coming to rest quietly.

"Well," said the insurance man, "if you had hit the pier, if you had hit a boat, if you had capsized a fisherman, if you had damaged the embankment, if...you'd be covered. But what your boat did was dig up somebody's expensive lawn. Ashore. You're just not covered for that."

Or...if it had only been an opossum instead of a raccoon...if only your sleeve had caught on the handle instead of the screen...if only the bird had been inside the house...if only the man had shot you instead of pushing the boxes over on you...

A law of nature, perhaps, that causes only those things to happen for which your expensive insurance does not cover you.

Maybe they will get that terminal repaired some day.

# Naaaah....
# Couldn't Be True

Some reports of events that got out of the control of the people who started them leave questions in the mind. Surely, some of these things can't be true, but the stories persist. May be worth noting a couple of floating tales, so that when they float by again, in altered form, we may compare the details. For example.:

You've landed on the moon in Eagle. You are the first folks there, and the world is watching, listening, savoring the whole experience. Very difficult for you to achieve any privacy.

Those space suits with backpacks, tools, and helmets, are terribly clumsy, and you bump into everything as you move about, or as you worm your way into and out of the garments.

During one of the struggles with this stuff in the cramped quarters, you bump some things that shouldn't be bumped, and you snap a switch off the controls, break the plastic lever right off at the base, so the switch can't be operated.

In the time remaining on the moon, you give a great deal of thought to this interesting little problem, and you discuss it discreetly with people in Houston, hoping to draw their attention to helping you solve the problem, without attracting the attention of everybody else in the world, because it's embarrassing, not a matter you want to share with just everybody. Still, time is limited, and you speak technical Pig Latin with the guys, so they can get moving on a solution quietly.

They do get moving in Houston. People climb into the duplicate equipment there, break off the switch in the matching cockpit, and give some thought to fixing it with only the tools you have on the moon.

They try this and that, chatting with you as helpfully as possible, under the public circumstances. Several ideas don't work, and you let them know about that, controlling a tendency of your voice to quaver a bit while discussing the matter.

Time passes. More time passes.

Then they call your attention to the pen you have with you, a ball-point pen. The guy in the matching vehicle in Houston has managed to work the switch in his unit, using a pen that matches yours. You might just give that a whirl. Don't turn the switch on, mind you, just see if it fits, and will work.

Yes, it looks promising.

So, finish up all the activity on the moon, put out the trash, leave a message for other visitors, close the hatch, and get set to go.

Go. There's the problem.

The switch reported broken in this drama is the one absolutely critical to turning on the rocket engine to lift you from the surface of the moon. No switch, no journey home. Nettlesome problem, bound to cause talk among the neighbors.

But the pen worked. You came back for a chat with the guy who designed the switch, and there's no gossip about the affair.

Except for this circulating story. Surely, they wouldn't have put the switch for take-off where it could be broken. People just don't do silly things like that. Naaaah. . . couldn't be true.

And there's a story about a chap who set out in one direction, but to his surprise, went another way. Pay no attention, bound to be just malicious rumor.

The great German rocket works at Peenemunde was a source of real interest to both East and West as Germany began to crumble, and there was some chance of grabbing a handful of German Rocket Scientists full of useful information.

A *gentleman's agreement* prevented either the Russians or the Americans from swooping in there, and kidnapping the interesting people, but gentlemen being what they are, various stratagems were employed to bend the agreement. (One distinguished scientist who figured largely in U.S. rocket development said that a U.S. Corporal knocked on his door at three in the morning, this inside territory still nominally held by German troops, and explained politely that an American truck would be traveling along the road in front of the house in fifteen minutes. He said that they might be willing to pick up hitchhikers. "My wife and I did not wait fifteen minutes. We ran out to the road in our nightclothes, and hitched a ride in an American truck. It was a long ride. I traveled all the way to White Sands from Peenemunde.") Indeed, unofficial little filibustering parties from various organizations without central coordination ran in to snatch various key people. Some reports suggest that different raiding parties exchanged shots while contending for their game. They wouldn't really do that, would they?

One of the participants in these affairs occasionally sighs while reading the news of the day, looks thoughtful, and slowly recounts the following story.

"I was in a three-man team assigned to bring out Wernher von Braun. There was a lot of confusion in the area, with people from various armies running back and forth, and little groups like ours ignoring everything else while bound on a special task.

"The intelligence people had good information. Our route was perfectly clear, and everything was where they said it would be. We found our man with no big problem. He was all dressed, packed, ready to go.

"The only problem was that he didn't want to go with us. He was headed in the other direction, East. I explained to him that his travel plans had been altered, but he was very insistent. We had to drag him along, just to have a useful conversation about the matter.

HIS TRAVEL PLANS HAD BEEN ALTERED.

"While we were having the conversation, a sniper opened up on us, and shot my Sergeant dead. This inhibited our discussion a good bit, because we had to deal with this new matter. Our man probably figured that we wouldn't shoot him, because we were supposed to bring him back alive. Dead German Rocket Scientists may seem like a good thing while they are actively dropping bombs on London, but circumstances alter cases, and living German Rocket Scientists were the day's fashion. Ours not to reason why.

"So we had to do something with a not-very-frightened scientist while we dealt with the sniper. We tied von Braun to a tree, is what we did. He disapproved of this strongly, and during the debate, his arm was broken.

"We did what was necessary to kill the sniper, but not before he had shot me in the leg. That not only made it hard to walk rapidly; it tried my patience. My sense of humor was gone by the time we untied von Braun, and I don't suppose he enjoyed our trip back to our side.

"Maybe he thought we were somebody else, really Russians pretending to be Yanks, and he faked his desire to go East. Maybe pigs can fly."

This must be a fabrication built around an interesting circumstance. Dig out your books on the history of space travel, and you'll find chapters on the gathering of German Rocket Scientists from Peenemunde. In several places you will see printed a picture of Dr. von Braun with a great smile, and great big cast on his broken arm, happily joining the forces of sweetness and light in the West. Gives a body a turn.

# R&D is Catching

There was a nice little cannery, years ago, that made good products, ran entertaining ads on television, and prospered. The proprietors decided to spend a bit of their earnings on Research and Development—chiefly development, which is considered rather less risky—to make better products for an exciting world. There's no such thing as a "little bit of research and development." Once you're hooked, you're hooked.

Maybe these folks are still around. If you find them, you'll be charmed.

Their major project was a new sort of helicopter. Canned peaches to helicopters is no great leap. They created the strangest looking helicopter in town, built three or four of them in various sizes. They looked like big boots, streamlined, modern, functional, but like big boots.

The rotors stuck up above the boot tops, and the pilot and passengers rode in the cabin forward of the rotor. Cows, sheep, and telephone linemen scattered as these strange vehicles came skimming over the hills.

A little more money, a little more time, a little more effort, a few nights without sleep, a few more nights without sleep, a few . . . zzzzzzzzzzzzzz . . . . . . . .

Then the project stopped when a government inspector was killed in a crash along with the test pilot. Pity. It's bad to let the Feds who are supposed to approve your

A NEW SORT OF HELICOPTER

design go down with the ship. The project crashed with the plane.

...but they had something else to keep them fascinated. Have you ever thought about how they put the word "Sunkist" on an orange or a lemon? No? Well few of us have, or care. It's no big deal with citrus fruits that have firm, thick skins to stamp a legend on the fruit in non-toxic ink or dye. No sleepless nights here.

Now, think on strawberries.

It seems that marketing people are wild about the idea of printing some identifying word on strawberries. If "Sunkist" has done marvels for citrus marketing, "Hivemaker" or some such label might do the same for strawberries. Minds boggle, palms itch, and hearts flutter at the very idea, apparently.

But how do you print on a strawberry?

You can't even touch a strawberry without doing it injury of some kind, and the folks who pick strawberries are even required to wear gloves, it is said. The gentle touch of a bare finger will cause a fungus to appear as if by magic on the surface of a luscious berry, rendering it unfit for market, with all of its companions in the carton. Print on that?

Well, they had an approach, and it too consumed money at a ferocious rate, while entertaining the researchers.

The scheme was to xerox the berries, sort of. That is, they had an electrostatic process that could put powder in  specified pattern on almost anything. Indeed, *Time* magazine ran a picture of a label that had been put on a raw egg on a plate. (No, not on the shell, on the raw yolk and white lying right there on the plate.) "We can print on still water," said the proud innovators who had developed the basic technology.

And they could, too. They could do more amazing things than that. They could print perfectly good letters on the far side of a pencil or a pipe, or on the extremely rough surface of a concrete block. How's that?

Really, the toner was poofed out through a little screen by a blast of air. Strong electrostatic fields grabbed the particles of toner, and carried them right where they were supposed to go. If you held a pencil or a small piece of pipe next to the screen, and pushed the botton, the stuff would poof out on command, and wrap itself right around the pencil, printing letters as neatly on the side away from the screen as on the side toward it. Astounding.

A winner, no?

Well, yes and no.

It's all very well to place a pattern of powdered toner on a surface. It's something else to make it stay there. Xerox used to have two processes for making the toner stick. One involved exposing the paper with the toner on it to ammonia fumes that would dissolve the stuff, or something, and make it cling to the paper. When it was dry, it stuck nicely, letting you read what was written after your tears stopped flowing from the fumes.

The other approach, the one in use today in most of the machines, is to bake the toner onto the surface. That's why the machine is hot, and why the copies char so interestingly when they get stuck in the machine. (The Model 813 used to eat your original document and burn it up with the copy once in a while. Hooray for progress.)

So what are you going to do with the strawberry that faints if you look at it too hard? Pencils, pipes, and firebricks can stand fumes and ovens. Strawberries can't stand much of anything. They could poof the magic words onto the surface of the fruit, but they wouldn't stay. And they wouldn't stay, and they wouldn't stay. No point in dreaming of cherries, rutabagas, and blueberries until the strawberries would hold the print. Lettuce? Carrots, Kale, Lima Beans? Tobacco? Wheat? Have you a vision of each little flat oat imprinted with the smiling face of a long-haired old guy in a funny hat? Yes, these wonders may yet be . . . but first the strawberries.

Where is the project now?

Perhaps somebody knows.

Perhaps some excitement-driven innovator with an odd light in his eyes is even now holding up one strawberry after another to be poofed with a magic word, then subjected to a test process for fixing the toner. Has somebody developed a toner that is not itself a pigment, but will cause the strawberry itself to turn black where the toner touches it, creating a permanent mark without further treatment?

Well, back to the cannery . . . but keep an eye on the grapes. Somebody must still be at it. These things get a grip on your soul.

# Ready When You Are, C.B.

The industrial film about rock crushers called for a very dramatic opening shot. The camera was to hold on the clear sky for thirty seconds so the viewers could admire a long quotation in white type overlaid against the azure. When the noble sentiment—something about how hard it was to break rocks in olden times, and how much better things are getting now—had been absorbed completely, the camera was to tilt down from the sky to look at a huge limestone cliff across the quarry at whose edge the camera was sitting. After a couple of seconds, that rock face was to collapse in an immense explosion. As the chunks of rock toppled to the quarry floor, and the billows of dust rose in great clouds, the film's main title would appear, supported by a fine burst of music. Elegant.

Also a bit touchy to shoot.

First you have to go to Central Indiana with a film crew in midsummer. Some obscure natural law compels summertime visits to the limestone quarries so that the film will melt in the magazines and crew members will sag senseless to the floor of the quarry in the heat. The sun penetrates the soggy air to reverberate fiercely off the white rock walls. You have all night to get over the sunstroke, and plenty of rest. Except for sleazy roadhouses, Indiana closes at five-thirty in the afternoon. This general environment encourages error.

More, they don't blast at the quarry every day. Indeed, they spend a month, laboriously boring holes in the limestone some yards back from the edge of the face. They pack some explosive into the holes one day, and shoot it off. This causes a large number of pieces of stone, big and little, to fall to the bottom of the quarry. While the blasting crew drills some more nice holes over the next month, other people pick up the rock, and do whatever it is they do with chunks of limestone. Then another shot, and another happy month of picking up the pieces.

What that means to the film crew is that they'd better be present on the right day with their equipment, and they'd better get it right or it's another expensive trip back to the quarry a month later.

The director was a bit tense about his responsibility the day of the shot. He had added reason to be tense, since the sky was not plain, simple blue, but was provided liberally with clouds. The camera was ready; the sound gear was ready. The director fidgeted as everybody waited hopefully for one whole minute of clear sky and bright sunshine among the drifting clouds.

"I think there's an adequate hole coming," said the cameraman, "and I don't see any after it for a long time."

"We'll do it," said the director. "Get ready. You're sure it's a big enough hole?"

"Yes, I think so."

"You're sure of the move?"

"Yes, tried it several times."

"And you're racked over?"

"Yep, I even have film in the camera."

"Never mind the comedy, just get the pictures. You sure there's power to the recorders over there?"

"Yes, we're already rolling, got plenty of tape."

"Well don't roll until I say so. We don't know what's gonna happen, and I don't want to have to reload at the last second."

"O.K., it's off."

"Keep those reflectors on the rocks, we've got to be able to see it clearly when we tilt down."

"Right, we're all set, no problem."

"Are you sure the camera's racked over?"

"Don't worry, we're all set here."

Having nagged his crew as much as he dared, the director cast around for something else to check. He remembered the quarry man next to him, and another worry crossed his mind.

"Are you sure that your blasting crew knows the signal to fire the shot? We have to time this just right."

"Don't worry," said the quarry man reassuringly. "All I have to do is raise my arms, like this."

He raised his arms in the agreed fashion.

KABOOOOOOOM!

It was a beautiful blast. In anticipation of the moviemaking, the blasting crew had dropped in a few extra pinches of explosive, just for good measure. Beautiful. Chunks of rock flew high in the air, arcing gracefully up, up, over the quarry.

The film crew stared. The camera did not roll. The sound did not roll. The quarry man stared with them.

"DON'T WORRY," SAID THE QUARRYMAN.

The rocks reached the top of their trajectory, and sailed gracefully back down, all around the folks. Oddly, not on top of anybody.

"It didn't occur to anybody to move away from the falling rocks as they bounced off our vehicles and equipment. We were stupefied, gazing at what should have been our wonderful picture. It was great."

It was great a month later, too, when they went back to do it all over. This time the director gave his own signal to the blasting crew. The nice quarry man just waited at the crusher, sitting on his hands.

# Party Time

The purpose was to increase production.

A nice side effect was the opportunity to spread a little light and cheer in a charming public relations gesture.

The company was opening a new processing plant on the Indian reservation, a nice new mill. New mills didn't come along all that often, and it seemed important to mark the point, cement relations with the local folks, win new friends, disarm old enemies. Besides, everybody likes parties, and this was to be a dandy.

It featured barbecued beef and soda pop.

Word went out, and the guests began to gather. They rode in on horseback, in wagons, in pickup trucks. They walked, pedaled bicycles, hitched rides on company trucks. Individuals came, families came, whole communities came. Hundreds of people drifted in from the remotest canyons of the reservation, all determined to cement relations.

Indeed, the turnout was greater by far than expected, and before many hours had passed, the supply of soda pop was running dangerously low. Searching parties were sent out for more.

On the second day, the supply of beef began to run low. Nobody was in danger of starvation, because the well-organized celebrants had brought food with them, and the temporary city that had formed around the new

mill featured scores of cooking fires. Beef was the item
of choice, however, and hunters were sent every direction to find cattle. They did find cattle, and brought
them back, though successive parties were forced to
travel farther and longer.

A crisis developed on the third day, when supplies of
fuel ran short, but resourceful firemakers solved the
problem by taking some of the obviously excess wood
wasted on the construction of the mill. A board here, a
post there.

RESOURCEFUL FIREMAKERS SOLVED THE PROBLEM.

The drovers managed to find beef enough. Tankers of
soda pop arrived with refreshing regularity. The wood-
cutters kept up with the insatiable fires, and the
barbecue raged on.

All good things come to an end. On the fifth day the
energy of the celebrants began to flag, the tankers were
reduced in number, and cattle were getting scarcer. The
party broke up, and people streamed away to their
various pursuits, leaving a quiet place where there had
been loud and delightful activity.

Oh yes, the supply of wood had run out, too. The mill
had been stripped, chopped, and burned. Very little re-

mained but the metal elements and the foundation. The company officials gazed dismally at the ruins, brooding over the effect on production, but warmed by the evident success of the barbecue.

Yes, they rebuilt the mill, but thoughtfully suppressed news of the scheduled opening. A little PR goes a long way.

# Hail Fellow

"In Germany, it was part of your pay to be addressed by your full title," said Dr. Schmidt over a beer. "I was Herr Professor Doktor Schmidt, and would have been mortally offended if an employee under my direction had failed to give me my full due, no matter how much time it took away from getting any work done.

"But we lost the war, and I came to work in the United States. From prisoner-of-war to GS-13 isn't bad. Things are different here. All those titles are just in the way.

"I had one American working in my group, brought in from some institution like Bell Labs, who was addicted to using titles. I tried for months to get him to relax, to stop worrying about his status, but it was not easy to do. He could not force himself to call me 'Wolfgang,' but must say 'Dr. Schmidt.' Poor fellow, he was stiff, worried, and was not working with his associates as well as he could. I tried very hard to make him relax, I gave orders, pleaded, threatened, but he would not do it. This went on incessantly.

"The laboratory where we were working was very secret, and the security people were in control of our lives in many ways. They even controlled the life of the president of the company, and forced him to do things he did not enjoy. For example, if somebody committed a security infraction like leaving a classified paper out on a desk overnight, the company flew its flag at half mast, and the president personally delivered a security lecture to the offender. The president hated this so much that the people who got the lecture hated it even more.

"One Monday morning I came into my office about ten minutes to eight, and was met by my secretary, who told me that I was a bad man. I had not left a paper on my desk; I had put all my papers away properly in my safe, and I had closed the safe. Unfortunately, I had not locked the safe, and the security people discovered that when they checked. The flag I had seen at half mast that morning was for me. The president of the company, who was ordinarily a very pleasant man, was waiting in my office to tell me how bad I really was, and how I should behave in the future.

"I went into the office, and sat at my desk to take my medicine from the nice man who hated to give it to me. We closed the door so that my secretary would not be embarrassed.

"During that same weekend, my uncomfortable subordinate had worked very hard to relax himself, and to show that he could fit into our informal, but hardworking little group. I do not know whether he drank a lot, or had a religious conversion, or hypnotized himself, but he succeeded with immense effort in getting up the courage to treat me as a friend. He decided to strike when the iron was hot, so to speak, to say something informal to me as soon as possible.

"He walked boldly down the hall at eight o'clock, walked past my secretary, threw open my office door, and shouted out jovially, 'Well, good morning, Wolfgang, you old asshole. Are you sober this early in the week?' I looked at him from behind my desk with great interest. Then the president of the company turned to look at him with great interest. We looked for a few moments, while the man who had taught himself to relax had an opportunity to identify his audience. Then he closed the door and went to his own office.

"That may be the only time in his life he ever relaxed. It was years ago, and he still calls me Dr. Schmidt."

HE DECIDED TO SAY SOMETHING INFORMAL.

# "And Leave the Driving..."

People working on advanced degrees in great universities probably learn more from the struggle to earn a living at the same time than they do from their academic labors. Robert learned a lot by driving large vehicles from one place to another while seeking further education.

"I was in Connecticut, trying to figure out how to survive the winter, when somebody advertised for a driver to take a truck down to Georgia to pick up a load of telephone poles. I applied for the job."

The company was naturally somewhat curious about the vehicular qualifications of the young fellow who showed up, but the shortage of other applicants made for ready acceptance of his report. "I drove trucks in the army," said he, figuring that anything could happen in the army. They were pleased. He was hired. They showed him the truck, recommending that he leave instantly with it. The poles were waiting.

Robert had never seen a vehicle of that size, close up. He wasn't even sure how to climb up to get into the cab, but his theory was that he might be able to get the thing started somehow, and out of the yard in some gear, any gear. Then, if he could find a quiet byway, he could experiment on more advanced handling of the truck.

Good theory. Good idea in fact. He managed to decipher the control mechanisms, and was soon happily

ROBERT HAD NEVER SEEN A VEHICLE OF THAT SIZE.

eating up the miles on the way to Georgia, miles and miles.

"It began to get boring, especially when I reached that area where the road becomes just a ribbon of pavement on top of a long, raised stretch of ground constructed in the middle of the swamps. I cruised along, faster and faster, thinking of this and that, dozing, driving, dreaming peacefully in my huge tractor, dragging the empty trailer. It was rather pleasant."

Then Robert's drifting attention was attracted by the appearance of something on the road in front of him. Gradually, that something become increasingly real, separating itself from the dreams, until his conscious mind perceived the thing as something to be dealt with. A farmer had quietly turned onto the road in front of the truck with a piece of farm machinery, and was putting along complacently. The machine was a wide one. Robert could not pass.

But he could overtake, and he was doing it fast, hurtling down on the rig. He began to go through the motions of slowing down, no mean feat, since he had developed no reflexes for this sort of thing, and had to think about every operation in succession. He became very busy in this intellectual project, still in his semi-dream state.

"I finally had a good idea," he said. "I was within a few yards of flattening the farmer and his rig, when it came to me that I could warn him by blowing the horn."

There was no horn button in the middle of the steering wheel, but he searched until he found a small rope next to his left ear. A lightning search of his memory told him that it was the control for a device that would emit a warning sound. He pulled on the rope.

"It was an air horn, and it made a noise like nothing I had ever heard in my life. It was one of those things that I failed to test in my original experiments. The horn was a couple of feet from my ear, powered by all the energy the truck had stored up on its trip from Connecticut. It had stored up a lot. The noise almost turned me inside out. I twisted the wheel convulsively, and shot off the road, making a magnificent leap into the swamp."

Robert's foot was pressed firmly to the floor on the accelerator, so that the vehicle did not just plop to a stop immediately, but surged on through the reeds and brush for a great distance before stopping. The engine died, and the truck began to sink slowly.

Stunned now by the silence and calm, Robert had only enough presence of mind to get out while the getting was good, and make his way from hummock to hummock, back to the highway.

The farmer had continued to roll serenely along the road, and was now out of reach or earshot. Robert squished a couple of miles back to a store that had a phone, and called Connecticut, collect.

"I've had an accident," he said. They listened with interest, if not pleasure, told him to give the police the coordinates of the sinking vehicle, and head back to Connecticut. They would find some other way to get their telephone poles.

"They even paid me," said Robert.

"What?"

"The law required it."

Perhaps the horn has been underestimated as a safety device by those who take it for granted. In this case, it clearly saved a life or two.

This knight of the road went on to other instructive automotive activity. On the strength of his experience with big commercial vehicles (leaving out the experience in the army), he got himself hired as a relief driver for Greyhound.

"I was in Berkeley, and needed to earn some money. They had a lot of buses, and needed experienced drivers. We were perfectly suited for each other."

As an extra driver, Robert had no regular routes, but was assigned on a moment-by-moment basis to take driverless buses to different places. One Saturday evening, he drew a distasteful assignment. He was assigned to drive the last special bus back from Santa Cruz to San Francisco.

A resort town, relatively sunny, on lovely Monterey Bay, Santa Cruz drew many weekend good-time-seekers to its beaches from cold, windy San Francisco. Greyhound was happy to take loads of people down there, and bring them back for a modest fee. The last bus, in the wee hours of Sunday morning, carried the leftover revelers, those who were too tired, too upset, too drunk, or too mean to catch the earlier excursion buses. The lonely drive up the dark coastal highway to San Francisco with a busload of malcontents was often a trial for the driver.

And it was this time. One belligerent drunk stirred up the other passengers, refused to be orderly, and tried to pick fights with those who spoke to him disapprovingly.

"I took it as long as I could," says Robert, "and we were just a few miles from the City when this guy began to interfere with my driving. Enough was enough. I saw a spot that looked like a good place to pull the bus over, so I wheeled in, and stopped. 'Do you want to step outside and settle this?' I said loudly, and I stood up. 'Yeah,' he said, looking forward to a chance to pound lumps all over me.

"I opened the bus door. He stepped out. I closed the bus door, and drove on. That's how to solve problems in the transportation business."

Robert delivered his remaining passengers to the downtown depot, put his bus away, turned in his stuff, changed, cleaned up, and was about to leave, when another driver appeared in the locker room, wild eyed, dirty, torn, scratched, and upset. This other driver was shouting, swearing that he wouldn't drive his regular route at night again without a gun.

What was his regular route? Well several miles of it involved local stops along the final miles of the excursion bus route from Santa Cruz.

"It was weird," said this other driver. "I pulled over to my regular stop just a few miles out, and opened the door to let a passenger out. Before I closed it again, a guy appeared out of the brush on the hill just the other side of the waiting area. He was out of breath, all scratched up, and out of his mind with rage. He pointed at me, and screamed that I had pushed him over the edge before he had a fair chance to fight me. Then he jumped on my bus, and attacked me. It was terrible. He was really beating me up before I managed to kick him back out the door, slam it, and drive off. For all I know, he's still there. The cops are looking for him. I don't know what he had against me."

"Well, I had my suspicions," says Robert. "We were all interested in locating the point of danger, so we questioned this driver very closely about it. Yes. The place I had pulled over with my drunk looked like a good place to stop a bus, because it was a bus stop. Distracted as I was, though, I had pulled so far over that the guy stepped out over empty space, and rolled down the hill. When he struggled back up through the thistles and poison oak, there was the regular local bus waiting for him. Marvelous. Actually, I didn't mention this to the

other driver. No point in upsetting him further. Really,
it's easy to understand. Nothing looks so much like a
Greyhound bus as another Greyhound bus."

NOTHING LOOKS SO MUCH LIKE A GREYHOUND BUS AS...

And moving on to other triumphs...

It was late at night once again; the relief driver's day
seems never to be done. Robert was pulling his bus into
the San Francisco terminal.

"I was glad to be there," says Robert, "because I had
drunk several cups of coffee before beginning the short
run, and it was time to visit the men's room to dispose of
some of that fluid."

However, the dispatcher came running up with the
news that a load of passengers was waiting for a driver
to take them to Santa Rosa, many miles north across the
Golden Gate. The dispatcher was eager to get the bus on
the road, and hustled the protesting Robert with his gear
to the vehicle, pushed him in, and ordered him away.

"Well," says Robert, "I had one scheduled stop in San
Rafael, and I figured I could last that far without actually
bursting my bladder. Off we went, as fast as I could
manage to make the bus move, given the hour and the
light traffic."

It was nip and tuck at that. Robert was gritting his
teeth, and moaning by the time he wheeled his sleek
vehicle in behind another in the San Rafael station. He

managed to stagger into the men's room and solve his problem. With lightened heart, proud of his stamina under painful conditions, and his grit in carrying his passengers briskly toward their goal, he strolled back to his bus, and wheeled it off into the night.

"We were several miles down the road when a passenger came up and asked me what time this bus would get to San Francisco. 'Gee, Lady, you're on the wrong bus,' I said. 'This bus is going to Santa Rosa.' I must have said this too loud, because all the other passengers on the bus jumped to their feet, and began shouting at me. They insisted that they had just come from Santa Rosa. Oddly, none of those people looked familiar to me, but I figured that my other distractions had kept my mind full, and I simply failed to look closely when they got aboard."

Confused, but persistent, Robert drove on to Santa Rosa with his riotous charges. It was only a few miles, anyway, as good a place to settle the matter as any. When he rolled into the station, that dispatcher came running out with his hands full of teletype messages from all down the line.

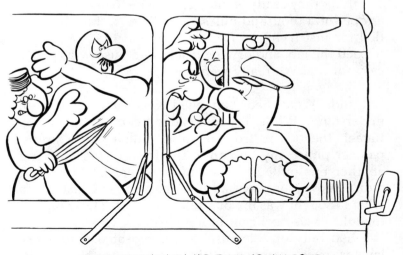

HE DROVE ON WITH HIS RIOTOUS CHARGES.

"Turn that thing around, and head back for San Francisco," said the dispatcher. "You took the wrong bus."

"I can't do it," said Robert.

"Why?"

"I'm legally out of driving time under ICC regulations.
By law, I can't spend another minute driving a bus until
next Wednesday."

It was true. They had to wake up a local driver, give
him time to get down to the station and give him instructions before anybody could take the bus to San Francisco. And Robert had to ride on that bus to get home. It
was his only transportation. All the passengers glared at
him during the wait and the trip, save for one who asked
if it was all right for him to go home again, and get some
breakfast.

"I couldn't tell him how long it would be," said Robert,
"so he just sat there, and looked hungry. It was not a
pleasant experience."

The following months were filled with unpleasant ex-
periences as the passengers threatened the company,
and the company threatened Robert, and formal hear-
ings were set up on every point of contention.

"I think they really wanted to drag me behind a bus on
a rope for a thousand miles," said Robert, "but they settled for just trying to fire me. I fought that, because I
needed the job, and driving trucks and buses was pretty
easy for me. We really went to it."

"Who won?"

"I did. What had happened was easy enough to
understand. While I was inside the building in San
Rafael, the bus in front of mine pulled out. The dispatcher pulled my bus up to the front of the line, and
another bus pulled in back of it, where I had been. I
didn't know anything had been moved, so I just got in
what I thought was my bus, and drove off. The company
thought I was negligent in not checking closer.

"I had only one defense, and I repeated it to every
lawyer, every company official, and every hearing of-

ficer at every opportunity. They all knew that what I said was true. Over and over, I said: 'Nothing looks so much like a Greyhound bus as another Greyhound bus.'" They just had to agree.

Does your driver look like a student?

Does he look as if he has ever been a student?

Maybe you'd rather walk.

# Shhhhh . . . .

Good luck with your conspiracy.

Those who believe in vast conspiracies must never have tried to carry off even a small one. Surely, dimwitted sincerity is a greater aid to getting some terrible thing done than is conspiracy.

Look, there we were with a little project that wasn't exactly secret, but wasn't exactly public information. It was just proprietary, sort of. The point was to keep track of some object that was churning and thrashing, cavitating and falling apart as it passed through a couple of hundred yards of water on its way to being buried in the mud at Mach three or four. Our project was to create a communications system that would work under water in these trying circumstances.

Came time to try it. Should be salt water, really.

Fine, where?

No point in going over to the ocean with those big waves and sharks and things. We can't very well go to a public pier where the water is quiet and deep, but people are thronging. This must be done privately.

Then where?

Go find some place.

Much wandering in a small car along the San Francisco Bay turned up a nice, still-water location where we could work quietly. It was in Redwood City, out there near the mound of salt.

So, we took our couple of pieces of bad-looking electronic breadboard up there one afternoon. The place was wholly deserted.

We shoved the stuff into plastic bags, sealed the bags, worked our way to a spot where we could dip things in the water easily, and dropped the bags in.

They had not struck the water before a police car rolled up behind us, and two grim looking officers studied our proceedings intently. A boat with three kids in it swung around the end of the quay, a derelict rose up from behind an old boat, two fishermen popped out from behind a rock, a pair of lovers strolled through our midst, oblivious to all but each other, and a helicopter landed next to the salt mound.

Nobody said a word to us. Nobody asked a question. Nobody did more than giggle as we tried to shove the floating plastic bags under water with sticks, and succeeded only in perforating them and getting the electronics wet.

We fished the stuff out, and tried to drain it and stash it in the car as inconspicuously as possible, while friends of the original sightseers arrived from Port Moresby, Samarkand, and Kansas City, attracted by reports of the show.

Later, our client asked sarcastically if we had also arranged to get our pictures in the local paper with the equipment.

"I have no idea," said Paul. "There may even have been television crews taping us. I couldn't see very well in the crowd."

Gad.

Good luck with your conspiracy, pal. We'll be there, about tenth row center, to watch.

WE'LL BE THERE.